American Fire Apparatus Vol. 2 - Aerial Equipment

Written by Wayne Mutza

Squadron Signal Publications

Cover Art by Don Greer
Line Illustrations by Melinda Turnage

(Front Cover) Hook & Ladder Company 10 of the Chicago Fire Department goes into action with its classic 1959 Mack B85 Special chassis mounting a rare German-made 100-foot Magirus aerial ladder. Chicago also operated a partner to this truck, along with two 146-foot ladder units, also mounted to Mack chassis.

(Back Cover) Milwaukee's association with Mack ladder trucks began in the 1940s and continued into the 1970s with this 1977 Mack 75-foot Aerialscope assigned to Ladder Co. No. 8, and Ladder Co. No. 2's "Big Stick," a 1972 tractor-drawn Mack CF Model pulling a 100-foot Pirsch aerial. Milwaukee's only Snorkel, in the background, was also borne by a Mack Model CF.

About the Special Series

Squadron/Signal Publications' most open-ended genre of books, our Special category, features a myriad of subjects that include unit histories, military campaigns, aircraft, ships, armor, and uniforms. Upcoming subjects include war heroes and non-military areas of interest. If you have an idea for a book or are interested in authoring one, please let us know.

Proudly printed in the U.S.A.
Copyright 2011 Squadron/Signal Publications
1115 Crowley Drive, Carrollton, TX 75006-1312 U.S.A.

ISBN 978-0-89747-629-4

Military/Combat Photographs and Snapshots

If you have any photos of aircraft, armor, soldiers, or ships of any nation, particularly wartime snapshots, please share them with us and help make Squadron/Signal's books all the more interesting and complete in the future. Any photograph sent to us will be copied and returned. Electronic images are preferred. The donor will be fully credited for any photos used. Please send them to:

Squadron/Signal Publications
1115 Crowley Drive
Carrollton, TX 75006-1312 U.S.A.
www.SquadronSignalPublications.com

(Title Page) FDNY's "Ten Truck," a 2001 Seagrave, which replaced the rig destroyed on 9/11, trains at South Street Sea Port. (Leesa Tara Ng)

Dedication

To Lennart Lundh, fellow historian, writer, and, above all, friend.

Acknowledgments

I am grateful to the following for their help in preparing this second volume of American Fire Apparatus: Dick Bartlett; Robert Brackenhoff; John A. Calderone, *Fire Apparatus Journal;* Patrick Campbell; Michael H. Erfert; Bill Friedrich; Steve Hagy; Bill Hattersley; Richard "Rick" Howard; Garry E. Kadzielawski; Dennis J. Maag; Chuck Madderom; the late Gerrit Madderom; Dale Mutza; Leesa Tara Ng; Dave Organ; Shaun P. Ryan; Richard Schneider; Patrick Shoop, Jr.; Mario and Trina Silva; Mark Stampfl; Jim Stevenson; Lou Tibor; Irene Wainwright; Venerable Fire Museum, Inc.; and Mike Wilson.

Introduction

The National Fire Protection Agency (NFPA), the governing body of the U.S. fire service, defines an aerial device as "an aerial ladder, elevating platform, aerial ladder platform, or water tower that is designed to position personnel, handle materials, provide continuous egress or discharge water." Numerous aerial devices based on this definition have developed as fire departments sought to cope with operations above street-level.

Unfortunately, tragedy is often the catalyst for improved firefighter safety. When Yuma, Arizona, volunteers rushed to a blaze in one of the town's few two-story buildings on 30 August 1899, their equipment could not penetrate fire spreading on the second floor. The floor collapsed, trapping and killing five firefighters. Shortly thereafter, the city council directed that ladders be ordered and that a hook and ladder company be organized.

Such hard lessons began in Colonial America when volunteer firefighters raced to the flames pulling hand pumpers and carrying crude ladders. Soon, wagons were pulled to blazes carrying multiple ladders and pike poles: wooden poles with metal hooks on the ends. Firefighters found the pike pole, or "hook," ideal for pulling at walls and ceilings. Wagons carrying hooks and ladders became known as "hook and ladder companies," a term still used by some fire departments. As the urban skyline rose and horses replaced manpower to pull larger fire apparatus, the hook and ladder took its place alongside the steam pumper and the hose wagon as a major type of apparatus.

As buildings grew taller and ladders longer, it became difficult to maneuver hook and ladder apparatus along narrow streets. The solution was independent steering of the rear wheels. Such tiller steering is still built into many of today's aerial apparatus.

Extension ladders became so long that they proved ungainly and dangerous. Injuries to firefighters prompted a search for an alternative. In 1868, Daniel D. Hayes, a mechanic with the San Francisco Fire Department, patented a design in which the base of a long ladder was fixed to a wagon. The ladder was hand-raised with the assistance of a worm gear, and a tiller seat was positioned below the ladder.

American LaFrance purchased the patent, improved the design, and in 1881 began offering its Hayes Aerial, in which the "bed" ladder was anchored to a turntable. The tiller position was relocated above the ladder to increase the tiller driver's visibility. The aerial was raised using a crank and worm gear, and it took several firefighters using gears and pulleys to extend the "fly" ladder, and rotate the unit. The device enabled firefighters to reach trapped persons and, moreover, it was the safest ladder in existence.

The most common method for raising heavy aerial ladders was the spring-hoist assist mechanism, which consisted of two powerful coil springs encased in metal cylinders. Then in 1902, Bedford, Massachusetts Fire Chief Edward F. Dahill developed an air-hoist for raising an aerial ladder. Spring- and air-hoists remained commonplace until hydraulic hoists debuted in the 1930s.

The second major type of aerial firefighting apparatus, the water tower, appeared in 1879 when John Hogan and Abner Greenleaf introduced a 50-foot pipe mast unit. Water towers were simple water pipes with a large nozzle that rose like an aerial ladder to direct powerful streams into upper floors of burning buildings.

By the beginning of the 20th Century, aerial apparatus, like steamers and hose wagons, had become so large and heavy that horses had trouble pulling them and the U.S. fire service grudgingly entered the motorized age. Two-, three-, and four-wheel tractors pulled aerial ladder trucks until a third major type of ladder truck, the city service truck, appeared in 1916. These units were designed to carry many ladders, but lacked a permanently-mounted aerial ladder. Although some city service trucks were long enough to require tiller steering, they evolved into a single-chassis unit.

During the 1920s, the quadruple combination, or quad, joined the fire service. The quad combined the city service truck and pumper, and included a hose load and a water or chemical tank. Quads protected areas that did not require an aerial ladder, ad were the first example of combining functions to save manpower and equipment. When an aerial ladder was added to a quad, it was known as a quintuple combination, or quint.

The introduction of fully hydraulic metal aerial ladders during the 1930s marked a huge step in firefighting tactics. To save costs, apparatus firms began offering aerial equipment built on commercial chassis. That trend, which continues today, yielded a wide variety of aerial apparatus, often bearing the name of multiple manufacturers.

Aerial equipment itself took on many interesting forms; manufacturers featured their own unique methods of constructing aerial ladders, which came in wood, aluminum, or steel. The working height of aerial ladders, which is measured from the ground to the tip of the fully extended ladder, went beyond 100 feet. As metal aerial ladders replaced wooden ones, they proved strong enough for the attachment of powerful stream appliances to their tips, ending the era of water towers.

Closed cabs, especially the cab-forward design, gained popularity in the 1940s. Aerial ladders, built as tractor-trailers, or mid-ship, were later rear-mounted on straight chassis.

The Chicago Fire Department's introduction of the articulating boom and the platform during the late 1950s spurred development of articulating and telescopic elevating booms. Aerial ladders serve as a continuous means of access to heights. In comparison to elevating platforms, ladders cost less, weigh less, and usually result in lower vehicle height. Platforms, on the other hand, are more versatile, stretch farther, can support dual master streams, and have a larger working area with greater load capacity. Nevertheless, ladders remain more common. Articulating waterway booms, a modern version of the water tower, are common add-ons.

Civil unrest during the 1960s led to the use of enclosed cabs for crew protection, and compartmentalization to conceal tools and equipment. As diesel power and automatic transmissions became more common, the budget-conscious 1980s saw a sweeping trend in rebuilding older apparatus.

NFPA standards imposed in 1991 have led to even greater use of commercial chassis. With the realization that budget constraints would become a way of life, fire departments have steadily geared their operations toward doing more with less, making multi-function vehicles more popular and aerial equipment dramatically larger.

Despite conditions that necessitate change, some things never change, especially the amazing spectacle of a massive aerial apparatus roaring to an emergency where firefighters meet the challenge.

Four major types of aerial apparatus do battle with a four-alarm fire in Milwaukee in 1981. Operating master streams from left to right are an aerialscope, a tractor-drawn aerial, a snorkel, and a rear-mount aerial on a straight frame chassis. All apparatus seen here, including the pumper and tractor-drawn aerial in the foreground, are Macks, indicating the department's preference for the type. (Author's Collection)

The most common and enduring type of aerial apparatus is the tractor-drawn aerial with tiller steering. Seldom seen by non-firefighters is this tiller driver's view. The tip of the fly ladder, which is painted orange for easier spotting at night and in smoke, incorporates a pike pole, or hook, fold-down steps, a spotlight, and a power cord reel. (Mike Wilson)

The Snorkel was conceived in Chicago in 1958. Fire Commissioner Robert J. Quinn saw the versatile articulating booms used by utility workers as a replacement for water towers. Aerial platform builder Pitman Manufacturing supplied Chicago a 50-foot unit mounted to a GMC chassis. Here, Snorkel Squad 1 (SS1) fights a major EL fire in Chicago in November 1962, just two weeks after the company was set up. (Author's Collection)

4

The Early Years

Soon after fire companies organized in Colonial America, ladders were rushed to blazes, first carried by hand and later carried on wheeled carts. Although the horse-drawn Hayes design eventually saw widespread use, early types could not be rotated, making their placement at fires difficult. Conrad Dietrich Magirus of Ulm, Germany, is credited with development in 1864 of the Magirus Leiter, the aerial ladder turntable upon which Hayes and other aerials were eventually mounted. Aerials of the Magirus Feuerwehrwerke were supplied worldwide, with only a few finding their way into American fire departments.

In 1880, Michigan volunteer firefighters asked inventor Fredrick Scott Seagrave to build a hand-drawn wagon with his specially made ladders. Seagrave was known for his sturdy ladders, which used wire trusses for strength. Many of Seagrave's ladders were sold to apple orchards. The following year, Seagrave & Company was established in Detroit and began building four-wheel, horse-drawn ladder trucks. Seagrave not only improved his design but he pioneered pumpers to become one of the giants among fire apparatus manufacturers. Eventually there appeared a wide variety of ladder wagons, their configuration only limited by the designer's imagination.

Tiller steering was an early feature of ladder trucks since wagons had to be lengthened to accommodate the increasing length of ladders. The popular Bangor ladders, which were produced in Bangor, Maine, were available in lengths up to 72 feet. A driver in the high-positioned tiller seat steered the independent rear wheels to control the entire ladder trailer, thereby greatly increasing the rig's maneuverability. The tiller steering shaft usually ran between the rungs of aerial ladders and ground ladders, so the shaft, and often the seat, had to be removed to use the ladders. When the men who pulled apparatus to fires were replaced by horses, riding positions, called running boards, were installed along the length of ladder trucks.

As ladder trucks were recognized as being equally as important as pumpers, fire apparatus builders who would prove to be leaders in the industry competed for their optimum design. In the 1890s, wagon makers Nicholas Pirsch and son, Peter, of Kenosha, Wisconsin, began building hand-drawn and horse-drawn fire apparatus. In 1848 they had built a wooden trussed ladder, which Peter sold through his own business, beginning in 1900.

Seagrave introduced a spring-hoist design in 1902 and American LaFrance followed with a similar design the following year. Edward F. Dahill's air hoist, which incorporated dual air tanks and compressors, proved far superior to the spring hoist in speed and control. When the firm Ahrens Fox, which had its humble beginnings in 1868 as C. Ahrens & Co., began building ladder trucks, it relied exclusively on Dahill's air-operated system.

As ladders grew stronger, it became possible to stretch a large hose up the ladder to reach flames on the upper floors of multi-story buildings. Water towers made specifically for this task soon proved even more efficient and safer than simple ladders, however. The first two Greenleaf water towers, which were horse-drawn and hand-operated, went to the Fire Department of New York. Other manufacturers also began building water towers, which were raised to their targets either by hand, spring hoist, or water pressure, with heights ranging from 35 to 75 feet.

As ladder-equipped fire apparatus came into their own as front-line firefighting units, they became a virtual hardware store on wheels, carrying much of the equipment that other apparatus types did not. Besides hooks and every variety of ladder, these truck carried buckets, ropes, saws, shovels, chains, and salvage covers, among other things. Axes, extinguishers, and lanterns were usually found on all types of fire apparatus.

Lanterns, which are often thought of merely as lighting appliances, are actually part of the tradition and symbolism associated with the fire service. Prior to the use of electric hand lights, beginning in about 1920, fire apparatus were equipped with several kerosene lanterns. Their globes came not only in clear glass, but solid color glass, and with glass that was half clear and the upper half colored. Each lantern signified a company type or a person's rank. Thus, the brightly colored lanterns moving about at a nighttime scene told firefighters where others were. Hook and ladder companies used solid green, while engine companies were identified by solid blue. Hose companies were solid red, hook and ladder company foremen used split green/clear, and senior hosemen were split yellow/clear. The chief engineer's, or fire chief's, lantern was split red/clear, while his assistant's was split blue/clear.

Firefighters in the 1800s took great pride in their equipment and spared no cost in outfitting their apparatus. Ornamental lamps, which were heavy, artistically designed, and had beveled glass front panels and colored etched side panels, often adorned rigs. These were commonly mounted as parade pieces. Intricate hand-painted trim and gold leaf were lavishly applied. Often, hood ornaments took the form of figureheads, much like those prized by seamen who similarly adorned their sailing ships. Pieces of fire apparatus were given names and affectionately referred to in the feminine form. Large shiny bells on apparatus, which were first used in Philadelphia about 1790, were as much decoration as they were an alarm-sounding device. The fire service, steeped in tradition, continues the use of bells on some apparatus.

The subculture formed during the early years of the fire service had its own lingo, much of which is heard in today's firehouses. Many of the terms are interchangeable, depending upon region. Firefighters assigned to ladder units, which were called "Ladder Companies" or "Truck Companies" became "Laddermen" or "Truckies." Some companies still go by the designation "Hook & Ladder." A large aerial ladder is "The Big Stick," while large nozzles attached to their tips are called "Water Towers" or "Master Streams." Hoses are "Tubes" or "Lines." Firehouses are called "Barns," harking back to the days when the revered horses waited anxiously in their stalls for the alarm to sound, or "Get a hitch." The list goes on.

Firefighter duties were already being defined during the horse-drawn era, falling into two basic categories: enginemen and laddermen. While it became the responsibility of the former to get water on the fire, it fell upon the latter to perform, most importantly, rescue, and ventilating, or "opening up the building."

As communities grew, and ladder trucks grew larger and stronger, their equipment inventory also increased to conform to the tasks of laddermen. New additions to the laddermen's equipment inventory included lighting equipment, life nets, ventilation units, powered saws, and the mechanical tools necessary to handle any emergency. Horses pulled ladder apparatus well into the 20th Century, but eventually they would surrender the field to advances in technology.

Often overlooked is the important role that horses played in firefighting. The smart and faithful work horses were revered by their handlers. Countless stories told by old timers provide insight to the fascinating characteristics and personalities of fire horses. The large white horse among these eight is handled by an equally stout firefighter. (Author's Collection)

One of Milwaukee's first ladder wagons is typical of the horse-drawn equipment that replaced hand-drawn ladder carts. Buckets hang alongside wooden ladders. The dapper volunteers hold bugles, likely the precursor to mechanical sirens and bells. (Milwaukee Fire Department)

Horses that pulled Boston Fire Department apparatus began to be replaced by motorized units in 1914. This three-abreast hitch pulls Boston's Ladder 13. The rig was short enough that it did not require a tiller driver. The company officer stands next to the driver, while firefighters ride the running board. (Lou Tibor/J. Hall Collection)

The American LaFrance Company positioned its horse-drawn aerial equipment against a large backdrop for pre-delivery photos. This hook and ladder unit with Hayes aerial was destined for Jersey City, New Jersey. Hand cranks, gears, and pulleys for operating the two-section, spring-hoist 65-foot aerial are visible at the ladder's base. Driver and tiller seats were simple platforms with rails. Below the aerial are extinguishers, lanterns, pike poles, buckets, ropes, and axes. (Author's Collection)

A three-abreast hitch was used to pull Milwaukee's Truck 4, an 1877 Babcock city service truck. All of the ladders were of wooden truss design and built in the department shop. Since the tiller steering shaft ran between the ladder's rungs, it was removable to allow ladders to be pulled from their racks. (Author's Collection)

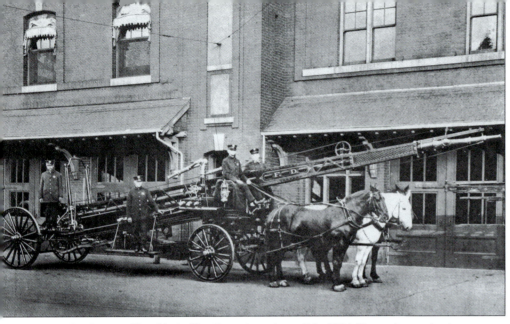

The Rochester, New York, Fire Department ran this 1904 Champion water tower as a first-response unit until 1927. The tower was hand-raised and extended to its working height of 65 feet. This was one of two Champion water towers used by Rochester, the other having been built in 1901. (Author's Collection)

Engineering experiments across the globe resulted in an interesting variety of aerial apparatus. This German-made, pneumatically-operated, four-section metal aerial was used in Pittsburgh, Pennsylvania. Another was in service with the St. Louis Fire Department. (Author's Collection)

Houston's fire department got extended service from this 1911 American Automatic 65-foot water tower. Beginning in 1921, the tower unit, which was hand-raised with spring assist, was pulled by an American LaFrance T-31 motorized tractor. A great deal of manpower was required to raise, turn and extend the tower. A turret, or deck pipe, is mounted on the rear of the tractor. (Houston Fire Department)

Gear mechanisms such as this were seen on early water towers and aerials. A hose is pre-connected to this water tower, the pipe-way of which was extended with the hand crank at left. Below the crank is seen a large piston which used water pressure to drive the large gears that elevated the tower. Water pressure, initially, was the main source of power for operating water towers. (Author)

This is the first of three water towers purchased by the Washington, D.C., Fire Department from 1901 to 1932. The Champion unit was hand-raised to a height of 75 feet. Two turret pipes flanked the tower and 12 inlets could be connected with hoses to supply water. The unit ran as truck Company 3, which remained in service until 1930. (Author's Collection)

Motorization

With the dawn of the motorized era shortly after the beginning of the 20th Century, ladder trucks, like pumpers, began to be pulled by motorized tractors. The International Motor Company (later Mack Trucks) is credited with delivering in 1909 the first motorized aerial ladder tractor. Straight-frame city service trucks, water towers, and aerial ladders were pulled by two-wheel front-drive tractors, while four-wheel tractors replaced three-horse hitches that pulled larger aerial ladder units. Prominent apparatus builders began turning out tractors, and by 1915, American LaFrance and Christie (Front Drive Motor Co.) took the lead in production, followed by Seagrave, Ahrens Fox, Mack, White, and Knox. The era signaled the beginning of ladder apparatus mated with commercial chassis. Most apparatus, however, would be built on custom chassis beginning in the 1920s when more commercial chassis became available. That decade marked the changeover from chain drive to shaft-driven power trains.

In 1923, Ahrens Fox began turning out 75- and 85-foot aerial ladders with air-operated Dahill hoists, a trend that it continued until 1939. Another trend begun by Ahrens Fox during the 1920s had ground ladders arranged in a double bank under the aerial. This lowered the overall vehicle height, allowed more ladders to be carried, and eliminated the need to disconnect the tiller steering shaft that ran through the rungs of ladders on city service trucks. Pneumatic tires appeared, which reduced the wear on trucks and eased the jarring ride caused by solid rubber wheels. Windshields were added and brakes were improved. To give ladder crews an extinguishing capability, many ladder trucks were equipped with chemical systems usually salvaged from chemical wagons.

Well ahead of its time, Peter Pirsch and Sons Company in 1928 built what is believed to be the first American fire truck with an enclosed custom cab. The following year, Mack Trucks showed off an aerial ladder that was raised with a power-take-off unit from the motor, which kicked off their production of 65- and 75-foot units. Hahn Motors of Hamburg, Pennsylvania also began producing aerial ladders.

The 1930s is billed as the Golden Age of transportation and in the fire service that was evident by stylish, art deco truck designs. Innovations in ladder trucks during the 1930s revolutionized fire apparatus. Pirsch would enjoy the lion's share, having introduced the world's first hydro-mechanical aerial ladder truck in 1931. Among its eight original features was the ability of one man to operate the ladder simply with levers. The 85-foot, two-section wooden aerial, which was pulled by a White tractor, entered service with the Spokane, Washington Fire Department. Then, in 1935, Pirsch developed the first aluminum alloy aerial and ground ladders. That same year, Seagrave showcased a 65-foot, three-section, welded tubular steel aerial. Pirsch, however, remained at the forefront in aerial ladder design, and in 1936 delivered to Melrose, Massachusetts, the first 100-foot all-powered, all-metal aerial ladder. In 1938, American LaFrance began offering 100-foot aerial ladders, which were four-section instead of the common three-section. This shortened the overall length of the retracted unit, allowing a permanently installed tiller position. Until the end of the decade, all aerials with a minimum stretch of 85 feet were tractor-drawn, tillered units. They would constitute one of three categories of aerial ladder, the other two being rear mount and mid-ship mount. Metal aerials were of steel construction, while Pirsch used an aluminum riveted design patterned after skyscraper skeletons that could move under stress. Despite the advantages of metal aerials, wooden aerials would remain in production for two more decades.

Adding to the decade's revolution in apparatus design was the debut of the cab-forward chassis by American LaFrance in 1939. After it was perfected and made available in 1947, this unique and highly functional design would become the standard for custom apparatus builders. Crown offered the cab forward in 1951, followed by Ahrens Fox in 1956, Mack in 1958, Seagrave in 1959, and Pirsch in 1961.

Water towers, like older aerial ladders, were converted to hydraulic power. Until 1936, a total of 102 water towers would be built in America by nine different manufacturers. New York, expectantly, had the largest number, 14, while Boston, Chicago, and San Francisco each had five.

Types of Aerials

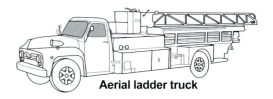

Aerial ladder truck

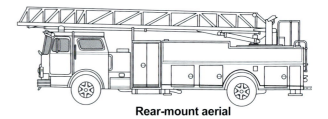

Rear-mount aerial

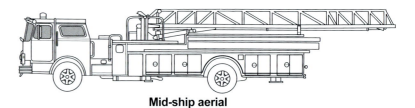

Mid-ship aerial

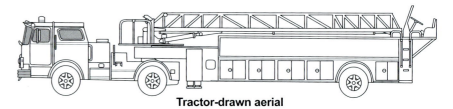

Tractor-drawn aerial

In 1909, Seagrave of Clintonville, Wisconsin, began turning out motorized tractors to pull ladder trailers. Initial offerings were chain-driven tractors with solid rubber tires, right-hand dri and four-cylinder air-cooled engines. This flashy 1920s model was given Seagrave serial no. 33171. (Author's Collection)

Milwaukee's second water tower, an 1889 Hale 55-foot unit, was manned by a crew of two and pulled by a pair of stout horses. The tower passed its acceptance test by throwing a two-inch stream a distance of 255 feet, while being supplied by a fireboat. Smaller front wheels maximized maneuverability of the large unit. Before aerial ladders were proved sufficiently stable, water towers were ideal for getting water to upper floors. (August Riemenschneider)

Like many major cities that used water towers, Milwaukee motorized its unit to take advantage of its usefulness at large blazes. In 1921, the department shop overhauled the unit and added a four-cylinder Seagrave tractor. By facing the tower forward, the unit remained a single chassis. A truss framework incorporating long steel rods and turnbuckle fittings helped support the tower's mast. Most apparatus bodies at the time were made of steel and seats were handmade of leather. (Milwaukee Fire Department)

After automobile designer Charles H. Martin joined the Knox Automobile Co. of Springfield, Massachusetts, in 1902, a few years later the firm began turning out three-wheel tractors for the fire service and the logging industry. A chain-driven Knox-Martin tractor pulled this American LaFrance aerial of Ladder Company 3 of the Lynn, Massachusetts, Fire Department into the 1950s. The three-wheel concept did not catch on and it was never used again. (Author's Collection)

City service ladder trucks, which carried ground ladders on a single-chassis frame, were used in areas where large aerials were not needed. This 1915 American LaFrance city service truck served the Prospect, Connecticut, Fire Department. Running boards were introduced on fire apparatus and became a popular feature of early automobiles. Grab rails for firefighters riding on the running boards extend along both sides, above the ladder racks. (Lou Tibor)

Ladder 1 of the Nashua, New Hampshire, Fire Department was the first Ahrens Fox aerial. The 1923 Model 85-6-1, 85-foot aerial featured ground ladders and solid rubber tires. McMicken Hall of the University of Cincinnati was a frequent backdrop for Ahrens Fox factory photos. This truck appears in a typical jack-knife pposition, which stabilized the aerial for raising and extending toward the outside of the angle. (Steve Hagy Collection)

This chain-driven 1917 Ahrens Fox Model M-17 of the Cincinnati, Ohio, Fire Department used an 1896 55-foot Hale water tower, which was raised by water pressure. This rig featured tiller steering and had two deck pipes mounted to the rear of the trailer. A truss framework incorporating long steel rods and turnbuckle fittings helped support the tower's mast. Like most apparatus built during the era, bodies were constructed of steel and seats were handmade of leather. (Dennis J. Maag)

The motorization of horse-drawn water towers extended their usefulness well into the 1960s. The New Orleans Fire Department motorized this 1893 Hale water tower with a 1919 American LaFrance tractor. Positioning the tower so that it extended over the tractor created a short wheel base, thereby ruling out the need for tiller steering. Inlets at the center of the truck's frame were hose connections for raising the mast. (Author's Collection)

The Portland, Oregon, Fire Department ran this 1916 American LaFrance Type 31 as Truck No. 2. Double-wall solid rubber front tires helped carry the weight of the tractor and ladder turntable. Steel rod rigging atop the aerial, which was kept taught with turnbuckles, served as a truss to support the ladder when raised. Manpower for major city ladder trucks in that period numbered from seven to nine men, with a crew consisting of officer, driver, tiller-man and firefighters. (Rick Howard Collection)

Built on a tillered chassis, this aerial ladder truck is a 1919 American LaFrance Type 31-4, with 75-foot wood spring-hoist ladder. Having serial no. 2708, it was delivered to the Mankato, Minnesota, Fire Department in December 1919. It poses in front of the Overland Company in Mankato, which was renamed Willys Overland Motor Co. in 1912. Willys later became synonymous with the Jeep. (Author's Collection)

In 1927, the Willimantic, Connecticut, Fire Department took delivery of this Mack AC-7 tractor-drawn hook and ladder. Its 75-foot wooden aerial was operated by a spring-activated, plunger-type hoist mechanism. Mack also offered aerial lengths of 65 and 85 feet in its AC line. Standard on the AC were solid rubber tires, chain drive, and searchlights. A nickel-plated bell is mounted beneath the truck's ladder rack. (Author's Collection)

This city service truck was built by Seagrave in 1924 and placed in service as Ladder 5 of the Kalamazoo, Michigan, Fire Department. The windscreen, which was fabricated in the department shop, was used on other KFD apparatus. A chemical tank is mounted behind the fuel tank, giving the crew extinguishing capabilities. (Author's Collection)

After serving the Pueblo, Colorado, Fire Department, this 1926 American LaFrance tractor-drawn aerial went to the Salida, Colorado, Fire Department. The 65-foot wooden aerial is complemented by banks of wooden truss ladders. Wide running boards are supported by steel rods. Unique is the rig's high positioned cab which offered excellent visibility. Eventually, departments either ordered rigs with cab covers, or fabricated their own. (Shaun P. Ryan)

After Milwaukee's shop superintendent observed a German-made Magirus aerial demonstration in Indiana in 1927, he convinced Milwaukee's chief to buy one. Built in Ulm, Germany, the rear-mount, 100-foot wooden aerial truck arrived in July 1928. Here, it demonstrates its stability and stretch, while unsupported. Through alternating changes to the chassis and aerial over the years, the rig evolved into an aerial truck that stayed in service for 60 years. (Milwaukee Fire Department)

15

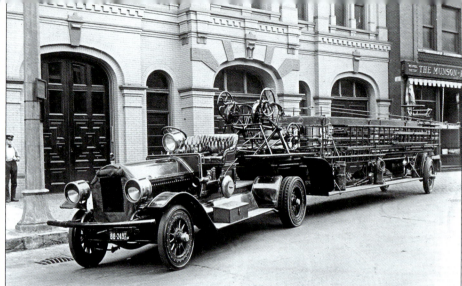

This American LaFrance city service truck, believed to be a Type 14 with chain drive and 105 h.p. motor, was the first motorized truck purchased by the Houston, Texas, Fire Department. American LaFrance built the Type 14 from 1912 to 1926. (Houston Fire Department)

Despite its use as a fire truck, this 1929 Studebaker easily retains its classic lines of the "Roaring Twenties." The Studebaker "President 8" city service truck was fashioned by the Wallace, Idaho, Fire Department, now called Shoshone County Fire Protection. A deck pipe is mounted immediately behind the cab seat and a life net is carried on the running board. Life nets, although necessary, were awkward devices, which made their compact stowage difficult. Eventually, they were made in a way that they could be collapsed into a relatively compact package. (Author's Collection)

Truck 1 of the Milwaukee Fire Department originally was a 1909 American LaFrance 85-foot wooden aerial. With the advent of motorization, its horses were replaced by a 1913 Seagrave tractor, and later this 1921 Seagrave tractor, which was a hose/chemical car. Below the aerial is a variety of ladders, including a pompier ladder and wooden truss 40- and 50-foot extension ladders. (Milwaukee Fire Department)

The last of five water towers used by the Chicago Fire Department was this 1927 Seagrave. Originally horse-drawn, the 65-foot tower was hand-hoisted with spring assist. After being motorized, the tower served until 1960. The unit could direct master streams from different levels, with two water turrets mounted to the trailer, and one in a crow's nest at the 40-foot level, in addition to the tip nozzle. A water tower's punch was limited only by the amount of water that could be pumped to it. (Garry E. Kadzielawski)

Like some cities, Milwaukee was known for its mechanical resourcefulness, which was reflected in its fire apparatus. From 1926 to 1931, the MFD shop built from the ground up 12 pumpers, six city service ladder trucks, and three hose wagons. Truck 15, seen here in 1929, was one of the homebuilt rigs. A large chemical extinguishing unit, which was salvaged from a chemical unit, was included, along with a large equipment bin atop the ladder racks. Although the shop-built rigs proved a huge cost saving, as they got older, parts were hard to obtain. (Author's Collection)

The Swanton, Ohio, Fire Department built this unusual ladder truck by combining a Pirsch 65-foot aerial with a 1937 Ford chassis with slab-sided body. Entrance doors are positioned at the rear of the cab. (Steve Hagy)

The Detroit, Michigan, Fire Department purchased two 1937 Seagrave 100-foot tractor-drawn aerials. The "S" on Ladder 3's bumper and signature grille were Seagrave trademarks. A control pedestal atop the aerial's turntable indicates a hydraulically-operated aerial. A roto-ray warning light is attached to the top forward edge of the enclosed cab. (Steve Hagy Collection)

Ladder 10 of the Reily Fire Company, Harrisburg, Pennsylvania, Fire Department used this 1937 Pirsch with 75-foot hydro-mechanical aerial. Pirsch aerials were built from clear-grained Douglas fir cut from Oregon forests. The space ahead of the tractor's grille is filled by sirens, bell, and warning lights. An ample supply of floodlights is mounted to the running board. (Jack Robrecht)

During the 1930s, Pirsch began offering a line of motorized metal aerials called the "Junior;" a 55-foot ladder, the "Intermediate;" 65 feet and over, and the "Senior," a tractor-drawn 100-foot unit. This 65-foot mid-mount Intermediate was built in 1937 with Pirsch's new riveted box aerial design. The truck went in service with the New Ulm, Minnesota, Fire Department. (Shaun P. Ryan)

This 65-foot water tower was built by Gorter in 1905 for the city of Los Angeles, California. The horse-drawn, water-pressure raised unit was motorized in 1921 with an American LaFrance two-wheel tractor. The tower remained in front-line service until 1958. (Bill Hattersley)

The Portland, Oregon, Fire Department used this 1939 Seagrave Model J-100 tractor-drawn 100-foot aerial. The Seagrave "J" Series was powered by a V-12 gasoline engine. Rear cab doors gave access to the rear bench seat. As ladder trucks grew and were powered by stronger engines, more equipment could be carried and more cabinets added. (Chuck Madderom)

Truck 31 of the Boston Fire Department was this 1931 American LaFrance Type 214 city service truck, which served into the 1970s. Controls, valves, and a pressure gauge below the cab indicate that a small pump was built in. A full load of equipment left little room for firefighters. It is likely that this truck was manned by only two firefighters, since the truck would serve mainly as an equipment rig used when combatting large fires. (Shaun P. Ryan)

Showing the stylish compound curves familiar to the art deco period, this 1937 Ahrens Fox Quad served Everett, Washington. Besides a full complement of wooden ladders, the rig carried a 250-gallon water tank and a pump rated at 750 GPM. Power was derived from a six-cylinder Hercules HXE motor. Ladders were rolled out of their racks in the enclosed body by chain-driven hand cranks. The rig was registered no. 9024 and served until 1978. (Bill Hattersley)

American LaFrance introduced its stylish 500 Series with streamlined hood and grille in 1938. This 1939 model with mid-mount, three-section steel aerial served the New England area. Such art deco styling made its debut during the 1930s and continued into the next decade. (Lou Tibor)

Truck No. 11 of the Corvallis, Oregon, Fire Department ran this 1936 American LaFrance city service truck with 500 GPM pump and water tank. Besides a full complement of wooden ladders, pompier ladders and searchlights were carried atop the rig. (Bill Hattersley)

After service with the Moscow, Idaho, Fire Department, this 1936 Seagrave with 65-foot mid-mount aerial went on to serve as Ladder 4 of the Colfax, Washington, Fire Department. How Seagrave's signature heart-shaped "Sweetheart" grille got its name is obvious. Single truck chassis proved sufficient for supporting 65 and 75-foot aerial ladders, with lateral stability for turning and extending the aerial made possible with stabilizer jacks beneath the turntable. (Bill Hattersley)

19

This 1934 Seagrave city service truck of the Marquette, Michigan, Fire Department featured a buckeye siren ahead of the grille, and a large water tank behind the fuel tank. Pin striping and gold leaf trim was an art form common on fire apparatus of the 1930s. (Author's Collection)

Truck 12 of the Bridgeport, Connecticut, Fire Department was a 1939 Mack Model E city service truck. With the E Series, built from 1937 to 1950, Mack introduced a variety of closed cabs. Pump controls just above the running board reveal the presence of a small onboard pump, probably rated at 500 GPM. (Lou Tibor)

Although bus-like in appearance, this is a city service truck built in 1939 for the Portland, Oregon, Fire Department. Wentworth & Irwin built the fully enclosed body on a Kenworth chassis. Wentworth & Irwin's work with bi-level buses during the 1930s probably influenced this unusual design. Located in Portland, the firm performed a great deal of body work for the city's fire department. The design protected equipment and crew from the elements. (Rick Howard Collection)

Although this ladder truck of the Augusta, Georgia, Fire Department bears no resemblance to those built during the early motorized period, it represents the evolution and longevity of fire apparatus from that era. The rig started life as a 1939 American LaFrance city service truck, to which an Augusta shop-built body was added in 1968. It was later placed on a new International Loadstar tilt-cab chassis, and the body remounted on an International 4900 chassis in 1991. (Dave Organ)

1940s

At the beginning of the decade, Ahrens Fox ceased its production of aerial ladders, devoting its attention instead to pumpers. Another mainstream manufacturer, American LaFrance, concentrated on a cab-forward design based on an experimental aerial ladder truck it had built in 1939. The result was its 700 Series, which became not only a classic, but the foundation of the firm's sole design strategy. The 700 Series was introduced in 1945 and production began two years later. During the 1940s, the stylish lines of the 1930s gave way to more purposeful designs. Most responsible for the change was the shift in manufacturing to supply the massive war machine. The war effort that permeated the country had a profound impact on apparatus production. Those that were built of necessity left the line wearing a minimum of bright trim, in keeping with blackout procedures and conservation of precious metals. During the post-war period, fire departments were quick to take advantage of the availability of reasonably priced surplus military vehicles for conversion to fire apparatus. Many departments had their own skilled mechanics, or relied upon municipal or local body shops, to do the conversions. By the end of the decade, apparatus manufacturers were enjoying a boom in sales as fire departments made up for limited wartime production. Tractor trailer ladder trucks were leaders in production numbers, as they slowly edged out the city service truck, in keeping with increasing requirements for fire protection in growing communities. Mid-ship mounted aerials, which made their debut during the 1930s, became more popular.

The decade signaled a departure from experimentation with the basic aerial truck, and began a period of improving upon established design features. Trucks grew larger as more powerful engines became available, which, in turn, permitted more heavy equipment required at emergencies. Besides hand tools, aerial units began carrying generators, portable lighting, power saws, and smoke ejectors.

Central Auto Body of St. Louis built this quad based on a 1949 Mack E Model for the Madison, Missouri, Fire Department. The rig, which featured a 500 GPM pump and 300-gallon water tank, served Madison for 30 years. It was unusual for Mack Trucks to have provided a chassis for another builder. The decade saw more use of white livery, which appeared a striking contrast to chrome and gold leaf trim. The application of gold leaf was an intricate and arduous process in which both artisans and firefighters took great pride. Using gold leaf is now known as a dying, almost non-existent art form. (Dennis J. Maag)

Truck Company No. 2 of the Quincy, Illinois, Fire Department was this stylish 1940 American LaFrance tractor-drawn unit with 100-foot aerial. Especially innovative for the period was the use of a four-section aerial, allowing a fixed tiller position. The name "Fred B. Werneth" appears on the trailer's frame. Large areas beneath the aerials of tractor-drawn rigs provided ample space for ladders and the variety of equipment carried by truck companies. The control pedestal for the aerial is located on the turntable, while opposite is the hydraulic lifting cylinder. (Steve Hagy Collection)

Lynchburg, Virginia, ran this 1941 Seagrave with 85-foot aerial as Ladder 1. The enclosed and extended cab featured Seagrave's "Sweetheart" grille. The fully enclosed trailer was locally built in 1943. Unusual during this time frame is the truck's enclosed trailer section, normally left open for quick access to tools. (Steve Hagy)

Mack Type 505 trucks built as city service trucks were rare. This 1948 example served Sioux City, Iowa, as Ladder 4. While ground ladders were pulled from their racks in the main body, equipment was stored in the upper open compartment. The mid-level step that allowed access to the equipment today would be considered an unsafe design feature. Basic pump controls and a booster line hose reel atop the rig indicate an onboard pump. Mack Trucks became known for its efficient crew cabs. Warning lights during the period were minimal, consisting mainly of red flashers. (Shaun P. Ryan)

This apparatus is historically significant in that it carries American LaFrance registration No. 9000. As the prototype for the cab-forward design introduced in 1945, it toured the country, and then returned to Elmira for extensive tests that provided ALF engineers valuable data to improve its line of apparatus. It was sold "as is" to the city of Jamestown, New York, in 1952, rebuilt, and during the late 1970s was sold to the nearby Village of Falconer. Old Number 9000 entered the 1980s completely rebuilt and diesel-powered. In 1993 it was sold to Cattaraugus, New York. (Dave Organ)

Bridgeport, Connecticut, purchased this wartime 1945 Mack Type 19LS to pull an older 85-foot wooden aerial as Ladder 6. Little chrome was used, in keeping with strict guidelines for conserving metals for the war machine. (Bridgeport Firefighters Historical Society/Lou Tibor)

After the popularity of the color lime-yellow wore off, few departments continued to use the color scheme. This 1948 Segrave with 85-foot aerial ran as Ladder 9 of the Bernalillo, New Mexico, Fire Department, having previously served the Albuquerque Fire Department. Six self-contained breathing apparatus (SCBA) are carried in red pouches on the trailer, along with a Homelite circular saw. (Shaun P. Ryan)

Boston's Ladder 27 was this 1949 American LaFrance Type 7-65-AJO, 65-foot mid-mount aerial. The firm built this "Junior" class truck from 1949 to 1959. Older aerial ladder trailers pulled by more modern tractors were a common sight as cities struggled to minimize equipment costs. Fire departments proved most able to extend the life of their vehicles, with some often surpassing 30 years of service. (Shaun P. Ryan)

Milwaukee took delivery of this wartime Pirsch with crew cab in 1945. Its aerial length was 65 feet, the minimum ladder height in that time frame. More modern aerials would stretch a minimum of 75 feet. Road sanders are visible in front of the rear dual wheels, along with a "Gooseneck" cellar pipe at the rear of the trailer. A hose was attached to the angular appliance for access to blazes in hard-to-reach confines. The three common types of fire extinguisher – carbon dioxide, water, and dry chemical – are mounted on the running board. Unusual is the fact that a few years after this picture was taken, Milwaukee began ordering trucks with open cabs before returning to enclosed types in the 1960s.

Two Pirsch "Senior" aerial ladders form an impressive arch in 1949. Tractor trailer units usually were jackknifed for stability. As an extended aerial's angle decreased, the more unstable the truck became. A firefighter's weight at the tip of an unstable aerial could disrupt the truck's balance or twist the narrow fly section. (Author's Collection)

Besides the color red, overall white was a popular scheme for fire apparatus during the 1940s. This 1947 quad was operated by the fire department of Miles City, Montana. Side panels extended behind the cab to house the 500 GPM pump and hose bed. Canvas covers often were used to cover uppermost equipment bins. (Shaun P. Ryan)

Between 1938 and 1940, the Bridgeport, Connecticut, Fire Department purchased three identical Mack E Series, which were produced from 1937 to 1950. This is Ladder 10's 1940 city service truck, which ran with Engine Co. 10. Loaded with equipment, Ladder 10 is typical of how departments exploited engine horsepower by using every available space to store equipment. Running boards easily became equipment shelves, leaving barely enough room for firefighters to ride. High cab roofs made Seagrave apparatus easily identifiable. (Lou Tibor Collection)

Compound curves and low, streamlined cabs were features of the 1940s art deco era. This Maxim city service truck served North Providence, Rhode Island. One of the common design features of such stylish rigs was compound curves at the rear of the cab section. The appealing lines gave the impression of separating the cab contours from the equipment-bearing rear section. Although major apparatus builders during the era followed the same basic body styles, each was distinguished by its own particular details. For Maxim, that included vertical framing of the radiator grille, a hood ornament, and squared fender tops. Over time, it became apparent to fire officials of larger cities that single-chassis (also called straight chassis) ladder trucks were too small to carry the standard equipment complement of truck companies. The number of city service trucks dwindled in these communities as buildings grew in height, requiring aerials that reached farther than the ground ladders carried by city service trucks. Most city service trucks were large enough to carry equipment that extended their capability. Such features on this truck include an enclosed pump, a hose bed atop the ladder racks, hard suction hose, a deck pipe, and search lights. Straight-chassis trucks of such length required stout frames, which eventually would be bolstered by tandem rear axles and heavy-duty suspension systems. (Author's Collection)

The Fire Department of New York operated a number of Ward LaFrance tractor-drawn aerials during the 1940s. This Brooklyn-based open-cab example was one of four 1948 models purchased to replace 1940 Ahrens Fox tractors pulling 85-foot wooden aerials. While most major apparatus manufacturers during the 1950s relied upon curvy body styles, Ward LaFrance stood by its simple angular style. The major benefit of such features was lower cost, which was passed on to the customer. (Shaun P. Ryan)

Pirsch custom engine-forward fire apparatus built from the 1940s through the 1970s was identified by long, tapered noses and horizontal grilles. This 1940 Pirsch city service truck served Pennsylvania's North Cumberland County. Peter Pirsch & Sons joined the style craze of the era, with one of its distinguishing features being broad, flared fenders. Headlights were faired into the fenders. Most notable was the company's signature grille comprising an array of horizontal chrome slats. (Shaun P. Ryan)

Completely void of chrome trim, this U.S. Navy Seagrave is easily identified as having been built during World War II. The 1945 truck with mid-mount 65-foot aerial was assigned as truck 1 to Naval Air Station Treasure Island, San Francisco. (Garry E. Kadzielawski)

The fire department of Roxboro, Massachusetts, ran this 1948 American La France aerial. The color white for fire apparatus began making an appearance during the decade, but did not become popular until much later. True to the saying that ladder trucks are hardware stores on wheels, this rig carries ropes, floodlights, a generator, and a battering ram, among other tools. Lying next to the aerial is a pre-connected hose and large nozzle for water-tower and ladder-pipe operations. (Author's Collection)

Rear-mount aerial ladders were a rarity during the 1940s, with the most sought after machines coming from Europe. One of only two such aerials in the U.S., this rear-mount rig was purchased by the Milwaukee Fire Department in 1928 from the Magirus firm in Ulm, Germany. Its 100-foot aerial retracted to a length of 27 feet, less than half that of other ladders. This compact size allowed a short wheelbase, which gave the vehicle great maneuverability. Nicknamed "Maggie," the truck underwent multiple rebuilds until it no longer resembled its original form. During a quarter century of service, Maggie served five front-line ladder companies and the training bureau. (John M. Hopwood)

"Big Green" is a 1949 American LaFrance 700 Series quint that served the Scottsdale, Pennsylvania, Fire Department. The rig retained its 750 GPM pump, however, during extensive rebuild, it was given a 1000 Series cab, and a 100-foot aerial replaced its original 75-foot aerial. Big Green and others painted in non-standard colors were proof that many professionals in the fire service were convinced that warning lights were more important than the apparatus color. Such deviations from the usual overall red, in their own way, drew the public's attention to the vehicle. (Mario and Trina Silva/ Antiquefirebrigade.com)

Truck 30 of the Belle Valley, Pennsylvania, Fire Department reflects the longevity familiar to fire apparatus. The 1949 American LaFrance with mid-mount 85-foot aerial was rebuilt twice during the 1980s and served into the 1990s until placed in reserve status. Painted orange with a cream-colored cab roof, the truck initially served the fire department of Warren, Pennsylvania. Bezel light units on cab fronts became an American LaFrance trademark. (Garry E. Kadzielawski)

After serving the Tulsa, Oklahoma, Fire Department, this smart 1943 Seagrave with 65-foot aerial went to Oak Harbor, Washington, and was assigned as Truck No. 2. Seagrave apparatus of the 1940s had distinctive waterfall grilles and high cabs. (Bill Hattersley)

During most of the 1940s and 1950s, nearly all of Milwaukee's 21 truck companies were equipped with Pirsch aerials that were both mid-mounted on straight-frame chassis or tractor-drawn. Aerials ranged from 65 to 100 feet. Despite the region's harsh winters, initial purchases of enclosed cabs gave way to open cabs. Milwaukee's Ladder Co. 15 was the fifth assignment as a front-line truck for this 1945 Pirsch with 65-foot aerial. (Chuck Madderom).

Even into the 1990s, this 1947 American LaFrance 85-foot aerial retained the classic lines of the 700 Series. Originally purchased by the Keokuk, Iowa, Fire Department, the rig went to Carthage, Illinois. Stabilizer jacks below the aerial turntable were stowed upright against the body. Wooden truss ladders are carried in racks below the aerial. (Dennis J. Maag)

For 15 years, this 1949 Pirsch with tractor-drawn 85-foot aerial served as Milwaukee's Ladder Co. No. 11. The control pylon on the turntable was a Pirsch trademark. Radiator grille covers for retaining engine heat, and road sanders mounted forward of the tractor's rear wheels were standard for Milwaukee rigs. (Chuck Madderom)

1950s

The "Fifties" saw some of the most dramatic changes in the types of aerial apparatus used by fire departments. Rear-mounts, most notably German-made Magirus units, made an appearance, although on a small scale. Mack trucks introduced an automatic transmission, although it too was not widely accepted. American LaFrance was in its heyday as the industry leader, turning out its popular 700 Series powered by V-12 engines. The firm's cab-forward design was adopted by competitors, one of whom, Ahrens Fox, announced its own unique design. Ahrens Fox's design would evolve into Mack's much sought after C Series when the firm purchased production rights for the cab. Other major builders followed suit with cab-forwards, including Crown, FWD, Maxim, Seagrave, and Pirsch.

Although builders made their aerial equipment more available on commercial chassis, with Ford's C Series being the favorite, the custom cab-forward had found a place in the fire service. Truck Cab Manufacturers, Inc. of Cincinnati became the largest independent builder of fire apparatus cabs. Through widespread use of their cabs by major apparatus producers, they became best known as "Cincinnati Cab."

Although Pirsch was one of the firms that enjoyed the boom in apparatus sales during the 1950s, it did so without offering a cab-forward model until the following decade. Instead, the company offered custom canopy cabs that provided protective riding positions.

The production of wooden aerial ladders came to a close in 1955 when the Fire Department of New York ordered 25 of them from the FWD Corporation. Wooden aerial ladders served into the 1970s, and wooden ground ladders were still seen on rigs into the 21st Century. The decade of the 1950s also saw the number of city service trucks dwindle as purchases of aerial apparatus increased.

The Chicago Fire Department is credited with one of the most remarkable innovations that changed the face of aerial operations during that decade. When Fire Commissioner Robert J. Quinn observed utility workers using an articulating boom and bucket device in 1958, he adapted the system for firefighting by attaching a large hose to the boom to supply a nozzle in the bucket. The design quickly won approval in the fire service, with Snorkel Fire Equipment Company setting the standard for elevating platforms.

The Snorkel's introduction and subsequent success paved the way for apparatus builders to consider aerial equipment variations that were not only unique, but stronger and could reach farther with more flexibility. Many of today's aerial innovations are the result of such experimentation. Since then, the age-old argument over the advantages of aerial ladders over platform devices has thrived. Not only are both types in production, in many cases their functions have been combined into one unit. Aerial ladders, although they provide a continuous path to and from a certain point, were found to be unsafe to move when people were on them, despite improvements made during the 1950s.

The rig that started the Snorkel craze in the fire service was this 50-foot Pitman boom mounted on a 1958 GMC. A piped waterway attached to the boom replaced the original hose strung alongside. The Chicago Fire Department labeled this unit "Quinn's Snorkel No. 1." (Author's Collection)

Pirsch was one of the last makers to offer cab-forward fire apparatus, having long had success with its engine-forward design. Pirsch workers hand-crafted the firm's cab-forward, thereby increasing its appeal. Distinctive Pirsch cab features were the swept angle of its cab-forward face, and the large squared fenders of its engine-forward.

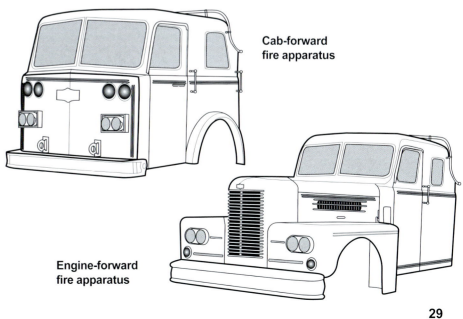

Cab-forward
fire apparatus

Engine-forward
fire apparatus

Although mid-mount aerials on single chassis apparatus was the norm, rear-mount aerials, both foreign and American made, began appearing during the 1950s. Firefighters found that facing the truck straight at the fire building and raising and extending the aerial over the cab offered the most stability. Any other position called for the use of stabilizers and extra caution. This was one of Seagrave's bargain quints, which not only used a 1957 GMC chassis, but incorporated a 750 GPM pump to augment the 65-foot aerial. Mad River Township of Dayton, Ohio, claimed the specially built truck. (Steve Hagy)

In 1954, the Pearisburg, Virginia, Volunteer Fire Department purchased a 1925 American LaFrance 65-foot aerial from Trenton, New Jersey. In 1956, the department replaced Ladder 4's tractor with this 1952 International Harvester. Then popular "Bullet" lights were mounted atop the fenders. (Steve Hagy)

The fire department of Downers Grove, Illinois, operated this 1957 General Motors Corp. commercial chassis with a mid-mount Pirsch 85-foot aerial. This GMC Model 630 proved to be a popular line for apparatus orders. Mated with Pirsch aerial ladders, the type proved less costly than custom apparatus. The company number 765 is carried on the hood and below front running lights. So popular were Pisrsch aerials that the firm's customer base extended far beyond the Midwest. (Dennis J. Maag)

This 1950s vintage Maxim with 75-foot aerial ladder served the Hamden, Connecticut, Fire Department. Tunnel style headlights, a distinctive radiator grille, and squared fenders were Maxim trademarks during the decade. A canvas cover was provided to protect the open cab. Apparatus buffs would quickly identify the Maxim aerial by the black panel with gold figures on the bed ladder. Equipment added later to running boards left little room for firefighters. (Lou Tibor)

White paint was commonly used during the 1950s for high visibility. The trend lasted with the Albuquerque, New Mexico, Fire Department, which ran this 1953 Seagrave Model 900T with 85-foot aerial. Extendable stabilizer jacks are visible behind the tractor's rear wheels. Red wheels provided an interesting contrast to the white scheme. (Shaun P. Ryan)

Boston ordered a number of Seagrave 100-foot tractor-drawn aerials from 1949 to 1962. This unit performed front-line duty as Ladder 26. Like most major cities that suffered civil unrest, Boston added protective cab covers. Although this rig has a covered cab, its tiller position remains unprotected since it had to be moved out of the way for aerial ladder operation. Locally built cab enclosures were constructed of weather-resistant wood or sheet metal. (Shaun P. Ryan)

Mack's C Model cab-forward introduced in 1957 was popular with the FDNY. Ladder Company 113's truck was one of 24 C85s with 85-foot Maxim aerials ordered by the department in 1959. New York specified painted bumpers and single headlights. Ladder 113's shop-built cab cover was a common feature on FDNY open-cab rigs. This cab cover used a clear plexiglas panel to increase visibility above the windshield. Similar protective enclosures protected the tiller position. (Shaun P. Ryan)

Mack Trucks had an agreement with Maxim to equip its trucks with aerials. An example was Boston's Ladder 5, which was a 1950 Mack Model 85-LS-1418 with Maxim 65-foot aerial. This truck performed more than a quarter century of front-line service. The 65-foot aerial soon gave way to the 75-footer as a minimum size. Diamond-tread walkways were placed atop cabinets and the rear fender. (Shaun P. Ryan)

Chicago purchased 12 1954 FWD tractor-drawn, wooden 85-foot aerials. The two-section aerials were manually raised. Ladder 13's rig ran with Engine 106 to protect the Avondale District of Chicago. (Author's Collection)

Ladder Company 135 of the Fire Department of New York ran this 1953 American LaFrance 700 Series tractor-drawn 85-foot aerial. The three-section steel aerial was short enough to allow a fixed tiller position. The absence of cab doors was common on open cabs of the early 1950s. (Shaun P. Ryan)

Extended to its maximum working height of 65 feet, Boston's Tower 1 demonstrates the simple effectiveness of water towers. The tower originally was a horse-drawn, spring hoist assist unit built in 1912 by American Automatic. This 1950 American LaFrance was one of three tractors used to pull the tower until the 1960s. (Shaun P. Ryan)

Ladder Company 46 of the FDNY used this 1955 Four Wheel Drive (FWD) tractor-drawn, wooden 75-foot aerial. It was common practice during the 1960s for the step areas of FDNY apparatus to be painted yellow. (Shaun P. Ryan)

Fire apparatus, typically, lived long service lives by serving multiple fire departments. Such was the case with this 1956 Seagrave Model 900-AB quint with 1,000 GPM pump and 85-foot mid-mount aerial. The rig was purchased new by the Clayton, Missouri, Fire department, and then sold in 1979 to the St. Charles, Missouri Fire District. St. Charles painted it white over lime yellow. When it retired during the 1980s, its aerial was removed and installed onto a 1959/1978 Seagrave quint of the Webster Grove, Missouri Fire Department. Such continued improvements ensured the long lives for most apparatus. (Dennis J. Maag)

Beginning in the 1950s, Ford's C Model tilt cab became the most commonly used commercial chassis and cab for fire apparatus. Van Pelt built the unit, which combined a 1958 Ford C850 with Memco 50-foot aerial and 750 GPM Hale pump. A 350-gallon water tank and hose bed completed the quint, which was powered by a Ford V-8 engine. The unit was in service with the Rio Vista, California, Fire Department. Air mask units are mounted atop rear cabinets. (Chuck Madderom)

The Alpha Volunteer Fire Company at State College, Pennsylvania, also known as "Happy Valley," home of Penn State University, operated this attractive 1954 Mack L Model with Maxim 85-foot aerial. The compound curves familiar to earlier aerial apparatus bodies is absent from this truck, due to the need to reduce manufacturing costs. Despite the design change, Mack rigs retained their good looks. (Michael Martinelli)

Seattle, Washington, ran this 1954 Seagrave tractor-drawn 100-foot aerial. The three-section aerial extended well past the trailer's rear wheels, requiring that the tiller seat be removable. Most removable seats were hinged on one side and easily swung clear of the aerial's lifting path. Drivers of such long-nose rigs developed a sense of knowing the position of the front bumper. (Bill Hattersley)

Kenworth rigs were long popular with Pacific Northwest fire departments. This 1950 city service model was powered by a Hercules gasoline engine. Unusual on this Seattle rig is a protective riding enclosure behind the cab, complete with window. The container for the power saw below the cab doubles as a boarding step. White paint provided an interesting curved design on the rear body. (Bill Hattersley)

This 1959 Seagrave 100-foot aerial of the Spokane, Washington, Fire Department was powered by a Hall-Scott gasoline motor. Hall-Scott was a major powerplant producer during the 1950s. The rig's chrome radiator shell was a hallmark of Seagrave apparatus built during the late 1950s. Seagrave aerial tractors were among the largest and longest built. Spokane soon switched to closed cab apparatus. (Bill Hattersley)

The Downers Grove, Illinois, Fire Department ran this 1956 GMC built by Pirsch with an 85-foot aerial. Screw type stabilizers secured below the turntable pivot downward for aerial operation. The use of commercial chassis and cabs often ruled out riding positions for firefighters. Smaller departments remained largely unaffected since manpower was usually less than major cities. (Garry E. Kadzielawski)

The stretched frame of this quint built by Central on a 1958 International R185 easily accommodated a 65-foot Memco electric aerial. Its pump was rated at 500 GPM and it carried a 250-gallon water tank. Water from the tank was drawn through a booster reel. The rig was delivered new to the Sea Isle, New Jersey, Fire Department and later went to the Hillsboro, Illinois Fire Company. (Dennis J. Maag)

The long snout and intricate grille of this rig easily identifies it as a Pirsch. The 1950 "Intermediate" 75-foot aerial served as Truck 6 of the Tacoma, Washington Fire Department. A Pirsch trademark throughout the decade was the mounting of headlights outside of broad curved fenders. Rotating beacons, then in vogue, were nicknamed "bubble gum machines." (Bill Hattersley)

Smeal built this Model C-801 with 1975 Ford C900 chassis as a demonstrator unit. As unique as its top-mounted control panel is its two-section, 45-foot Astro Star 45 aerial. The combination rig featured a 750 GPM pump and 250-gallon water tank. It is seen here painted lime yellow in service with the fire department of Ogallala, Nebraska. Since access to the aerial was difficult, steps or a ladder often were incorporated into large truck bodies. (Dennis J. Maag)

New York's Engine 251 ran with this 1951 Ward LaFrance 85T quad in Queens. Besides a 750 GPM pump and 250-galloan water tank, the long wheelbase rig had a full complement of ladders beneath its hose bed. Pike poles are attached to the body, and a makeshift canvas cover protects the cab. The wide variety of tools attached to the outside of this rig eventually were stored out of view to prevent theft and their being used against firefighters, who were once welcomed into neighborhoods as friends. (Shaun P. Ryan)

Milwaukee's Ladder Co. 1, a 1957 Mack Magirus, works as a water tower. At 70 feet in height, the Mack Magirus could safely handle nozzle tip loads of 220 psi. The truck's stabilizer jacks are extended and screwed down. A short ladder was necessary to climb to the bed ladder of the aerial. A safety rule of thumb for aerial laddders held that no more than one firefighter should be on a ladder section. This rule meant that a total of four firefighters could occupy a four-section, 100-foot aerial. (Gerrit Madderom)

The Milwaukee Fire Department was so fond of the Mack Magirus combination during the late 1950s that the department ended up having three of them. Department officials praised the rig's short wheelbase, which allowed it to fit into confined areas. Milwaukee did not equip the short chassis rigs with the usual 50-foot ground ladders since more reliance was placed upon the truck's maneuverability. The four-section, 100-foot steel aerial was strong enough that Milwaukee routinely operated them as water towers. Four recessed stabilizer jacks provided ample stability for the aerial. (Gerrit Madderom)

The Baltimore, Maryland, Fire Department ran this 1957 Pirsch 100-foot "Senior" in front-line service for 17 years, after which time it ran as Second-Line Truck 10. Pirsch introduced its squared fender design in 1955. Baltimore has long held the tradition of using this split color scheme for its fire apparatus. A loudspeaker atop the windshield kept the crew informed of radio messages. (Author's Collection)

The Portland, Oregon, Fire Department ran this 1959 Seagrave with 100-foot aerial as Truck No. 1. Portland, like other cities that experienced rough weather, soon began using enclosed cabs. Dual headlights were a common feature of Seagrave cabs. (Rick Howard Collection)

To replace aerial ladders on two Mack B85 Special chassis, the Chicago Fire Department purchased two Magirus 146-foot units from the Fire Department of New York. Although B Models, the chassis used Mack L Type cabs and hoods that saw use on logging trucks. New York had replaced the six-section ladder units with Grove 100-foot aerial ladders. (Chuck Madderom)

After serving the fire department of Wayne, Michigan, this 1953 American LaFrance went to Hinsdale, Illinois. Truck 442 featured a 1,000 GPM pump, 150-gallon water tank, and 75-foot aerial. Power was supplied by an American LaFrance 215 h.p. gasoline engine. (Garry E. Kadzielawski)

Along with the pair of 146-foot Magirus aerials it placed in service, Chicago mounted 100-foot Magirus aerial units on two B85 Special chassis. One was a 1959 Mack seen here as Hook & Ladder Co. 30. (Chuck Madderom)

Mack Trucks began making its popular C Model in 1957 and Grove Manufacturing began building aerial ladders in 1959. New York's Ladder 164 was one of the results of mating the two. The small number of Grove four-section, steel 100-foot aerials were easily recognized by their large, tapered bed ladders. An inclinometer near the rear of the bed ladder showed the operator the angle at which the aerial was raised. Ladder 164 was housed with Engine 313 in the Douglaston community of Queens. (Author's Collection)

This American LaFrance city service truck of Wethersfield, Connecticut, features the intricate gold scrollwork and chrome details typical of the 700 Series line. The series was produced from 1948 to 1958. Its successor, the 800 Series, which was built from 1956 to 1958, was slightly different in having a cab that was positions somewhat higher. (Lou Tibor)

Galley Brothers, a small company in Pittsburgh, built this city service truck for the volunteer fire department of Mount Pleasant, Pennsylvania. Unusual is the 500 GPM pump built into the front of Ladder 3's 1950 Chevrolet cab-over-engine. Gold scrollwork completes the one-of-a-kind rig. (Dave Organ)

Milwaukee's German-made 1928 Magirus, nicknamed "Old Maggie," underwent so many changes during its long service that by the end of its career it bore no resemblance to its original form. This interim version had the original wooden 100-foot aerial mated with a 1956 Mack B85 to serve as Truck Co. 21. (Chuck Madderom)

Seagrave enthusiasts would find this 1957 model's serial number, J-9700, useful in tracking its history. The stylish rig with 85-foot aerial belonged to the Alhambra, California, Fire Department. Unusual is a breathing apparatus mounted in a protective case immediately behind the officer's door for quick access. Open cab apparatus remained the standard for west coast departments. (Bill Hattersley)

Four new Seagrave 100-foot aerials are displayed at New Orleans' Eads Plaza during the early 1950s. Visible on the tractor-trailer rigs are swing-out tiller positions and chrome bells on the cabs. (Louisiana Division/City Archives New Orleans Public Library)

One of Maxim's first cab-forward aerial trucks was this 1959 model with 75-foot aerial for Truck 7 of the Terre Haute, Indiana Fire Department. The Maxim Motor Company built a wide range of fire apparatus in Middleborough, Massachusetts from 1914 to 1989. (Garry E. Kadzielawski)

Originally of the Lake Charles, Louisiana, Fire Department, this unique 1951 Mack 85LS served the Lake Jackson, Texas, Volunteer Fire Department. Resplendent in white with gold and yellow trim, the unit mounted a 65-foot Maxim aerial ladder. Obvious additions are a modem light bar atop the windshield frame and electric rewind power cords. Gold-leaf trim had been added to the comers of cabinet doors. (Dennis J. Maag)

Mack introduced its B Series in 1954 and the following year it became available with a tractor-drawn Maxim aerial. The rugged good looks of this B85, powered by Mack's Thermodyne gasoline engine, are accented by its chrome radiator shell. This 1955 Mack-Maxim with 85-foot aerial served Milwaukee's Ladder Co.12. (Gerrit Madderom)

1960s

Since fires were a grim aspect of the civil disturbances that swept urban America during the 1960s, fire apparatus design underwent lasting changes. Manufacturers would take their cue from urban departments that fashioned makeshift enclosures to protect firefighters. Cabs, riding positions, and tiller seats were enclosed, while compartments were added to enclose equipment previously in plain view.

Aerial ladders became strong enough to support tip loads, thereby allowing large stream appliances to be mounted to the tips of aerials. More maneuverable rear mount aerial ladders were tried, the first examples of which were imported Magirus (German) and Geesink (Dutch) aerials mounted on FWD, Mack, Maxim, and Seagrave chassis. Hydraulic stabilizers became available, although the transition from screw-types was slow. Diesel power became more common, especially in view of its reduced maintenance requirements, compared to gasoline engines.

The trend in elevating platforms continued, with the American LaFrance Aero Chief making its debut in 1963, Mack's Aerialscope the following year, and Calavar's "Firebird" elevating platform in 1969. The Calavar Corporation of Santa Fe Springs, California boasted the highest reaching aerial platform with its 150-foot model. A 90- and 125-foot model also were available, with the first Firebird, a 125-footer, going to Philadelphia on an FWD chassis. Sutphen introduced a fully enclosed boom, while Hi-Ranger open-lattice booms also became popular.

Since the Snorkel's two articulating arms were extremely long, Aerialscopes became more popular. Although their telescoping boom had shorter reach than that of Snorkels, their greater stability meant safer operating limits. The first Aerialscope constructed was a 1963 Mack C85F chassis with 75-foot Eaton/Truco boom delivered to the FDNY in 1964.

Philadelphia ended the decade with this order, consisting of four Seagrave 100-foot tractor-drawn aerials, two Oshkosh/Pierce 85-foot Snorkels and an Oshkosh/Pierce 55-foot Squirt.

The New Orleans, Louisiana, Fire Department shows off three new American LaFrance 900 Series ladder trucks in 1961. (Louisiana Division/City Archives New Orleans Public Library)

American LaFrance introduced its Aero Chief in 1962. This was the first unit, an Aero Chief 70, built on a 1963 International VCO-206 chassis. It first served Rome, Georgia, having been repainted yellow during the 1970s, and then returned to red during the late 1980s. The Aero Chief was retired in 1994 and traded to a Sutphen dealer. The articulating booms of the first two Aero Chiefs were styled differently from succeeding models. (Dave Organ)

The largest of the three models of Aero Chiefs was the Aero Chief 90, some of which used a tandem axle. This Aero Chief 90 quint was built on a 1968 American LaFrance 900 Series for Truck Co. 1 of North Olmstead, Ohio's fire department. Four outriggers were lowered hydraulically from their vertically stowed position at the rear of the unit. (Dave Organ)

Beginning in 1964, Mack introduced its revolutionary telescoping aerial platform. Called the "Aerialscope," the unit comprised a 75-foot Eaton/Truco boom mounted on Mack's popular C85 chassis. Although hundreds of Aerialscopes would be built, only 13 were built on C85s. New York received six and this 1966 example went to Butte, Montana. The unit served the Butte Fire Department until 2008, having been used on many large commercial building fires in Butte's uptown area during its first decade of service. (Bill Hattersley)

Firefighters often call ladder trucks "Hardware stores on wheels" and this rig, Truck No. 1 of the Ogden, Utah, Fire Department, was no exception. The 1967 American LaFrance 900 Series with 100-foot aerial carries a deluge set (master stream ground appliance) behind the cab, along with a pre-connected ladder pipe next to the aerial for water tower operations. The decade saw an increase in enclosed tiller positions. The light bar atop the cab is a much later replacement of an original rotating beacon. (Bill Hattersley)

During the 1970s, Ladders 9 and 25 of the Boston Fire Department ran this one-of-a-kind 1968 Diamond Reo tractor pulling a 1957 Seagrave 100-foot aerial. Riding positions for firefighters on this rig were limited, especially since a commercial cab is used and cabinets ran the length of the trailer in place of running boards. A deck pipe is mounted atop the trailer in the event the truck was parked at a scene in a way that allowed its use. (Shaun P. Ryan)

This 1961 FWD/Pierce with 85-foot Pitman Snorkel was obtained by Murphysboro, Illinois, from the Niles Fire Department. (Dennis J. Maag)

Mack delivered two of these unusual rigs to the FDNY in 1961. A six-section 146-foot Magirus aerial ladder was built onto a 1959 C85 chassis, giving the pair, called "High Ladders," considerable reach over standard aerials. This High Ladder was assigned to Ladder 119, which is housed with Engine 211 in Brooklyn. (Shaun P. Ryan)

Having begun as a wagon maker in 1875, Jac. Geesink of the Netherlands turned to ladder units for the fire service. The first mechanically operated Geesink aerial ladder appeared in 1935. More than two decades later, three made their way to the U.S., one each for Chicago, Milwaukee, and Cedarburg, Wisconsin. Milwaukee's four-section 85-footer was delivered in 1961 on an FWD chassis. Truck Co. 2's white aerial was later repainted gray. (Chuck Madderom)

This 1961 Crown with 65-foot Snorkel, appropriately, served Crown Point, Indiana. Crown apparatus rarely was found in Midwestern regions, having a predominantly west coast market. (Garry E. Kadsielawski)

Ellettsville, Illinois, operates this 1969 900 Series Aero Chief 80 quint. (Dave Organ)

Mack produced its popular C Series chassis for 10 years, and during that time the firm enjoyed a boom in sales. New York bought the chassis in large numbers and Milwaukee ordered 10, four of which were ladder trucks. Since the four C85s were mated with Pirsch aerials, the units were nicknamed "McPirschs." This 85-footer is seen at the department shop on its day of delivery in March 1967. In 1964, Pirsch began building its 85- and 100-foot aerials as four-section units to allow a permanent tiller position. (Chuck Madderom)

The Elko, Nevada, Fire Department operated this 1960 International Harvester Model VCO-190 with 50-foot Pitman Snorkel. Crown built the quint, which featured a 750 GPM pump and 300-gallon water tank. (Garry E. Kadzielawski)

Pierce outfitted this 1961 FWD with a 65-foot Snorkel for the fire department of Coopersville/Polkton, Michigan. Custom cabs that provided riding positions for firefighters were unnecessary in communities that used less manpower. (Garry E. Kadzielawski)

The Griffith, Indiana, Fire Department used ample labeling on its 1967 American LaFrance Aero Chief 90. The orange-yellow rig carried a 200-gallon booster tank and pump, the controls for which were contained in one of the side cabinets. All cabinet doors were marked with contents and featured kick plates. Nearly all articulating and elevating platforms, and their buckets, were painted white, allowing them to be better seen at night and in smoky conditions. (Garry E. Kadzielawski)

43

The University of Illinois, Urbana Fire department operated this Pierce-built 1962 Ford C Model with 85-foot Snorkel. The unit used a simple arrangement of flat railer and large forward cabinet. (Garry E. Kadzielawski)

Truck 19 of the Denver Fire Department was a 1967 Seagrave with 100-foot mid-mount aerial. This was one of five such units ordered by Denver. (Patrick Campbell)

Ladder 1 of the Barre, Massachusetts, Fire Department was this 1969 Maxim "S" with four-section aerial. The open-cab rig is fit with a canvas cover. A white radiator cowl gives this rig a distinctive look. (Dick Bartlett)

Pirsch began offering its much sought after custom cab forward in 1962, continuing the line until 1981 when it was no longer cost effective. Skokie, Illinois used this 1969 Pirsch with 65-foot Snorkel. (Garry E. Kadzielawski)

This Ward LaFrance/Hi-Ranger for the City of Groton was the first platform aerial in the state of Connecticut. Built in 1962, this cab style was named "Mark I" and was later changed to "Ambassador" when the cab's flat face was changed to an angular design. The 85-foot platforms were built by Mobile Aerial Towers, Inc. at Fort Wayne, Indiana. The lattice boom used a cable leveling system versus the Snorkel's solid bar linkage. Large sign boards bearing the department's name or the company's identity often were mounted to aerial booms. (Lou Tibor)

Mack open cab ladder trucks were less common than closed cab designs. This 1965 Mack Model C shows signs of modernization, having a four-section, 85-foot Kenco aerial, roll-up cabinet door, and reflective striping. This rig was the property of the Highland Hose Co. of Tarentum, Alleghany County, Pennsylvania. (Patrick Shoop, Jr.)

Truck 5 of the Gary, Indiana, Fire Department ran this 1967 Mack C Model with 100-foot Maxim aerial. The black over red cab scheme has long been popular with Midwest fire departments, however, Gary switched to blue over red during the 1980s. Stabilizer jacks are tucked into a well below the ladder turntable. (Garry E. Kadzielawski)

Glendale, Arizona, operated this 1968 American LaFrance 900 Series Aero Chief 80. It was powered by a Continental "M" 305 h.p., six-cylinder gasoline engine. In keeping with the need for maximum stability at the turntable, hydraulically lowering outriggers were mounted on each side of the rear body. Painted a different color than the body, these pivoted at the bottom downward for use. Their large square base that contacted the ground provided the best stability possible. (Chuck Madderom)

This one-of-a-kind rig was built by Coast Fire Apparatus on a 1965 GMC 6500 chassis. Its 65-foot aerial is from Grove, while its 750 GPM pump is augmented by a 500-gallon water tank. Truck 1 was operated by the North Central Fire Protection District, Kerman Station, Fresno County, California. The three-place cab of this truck was considered sufficient since smaller communities usually had less manpower than major city fire departments. (Chuck Madderom)

45

This 1965 Mack started life as a C95F pumper with the Rock Community Fire District of Arnold, Missouri. In 1986, L.E. Mueller Industries of Valley Park refurbished the unit and added a 50-foot Tele-Squrt, which came from a 1980 American LaFrance Century that was destroyed by a train. Herculaneum, Missouri acquired the rig in 1994, repainted it, and operated it until 2002. (Dennis J. Maag)

This 1963 Ford C1000/Towers with 55-foot Pitman Snorkel was purchased new by the Washington, Missouri Fire Department. It was sold to the Long Lake Fire Protection District, Pontoon Beach, Illinois, in 1984 and repainted lime yellow. During the 1990s, it went to the Lebanon-Emerald Mound, Illinois Fire Department, where it was repainted red. (Dennis J. Maag)

This interesting rig is the combined result of four major apparatus firms. A Darley 1,000 GPM pump unit and 85-foot Pitman Snorkel are built upon a 1964 GMC with bodywork done by Pierce. Its water tank capacity is 200 gallons. A Federal Q siren mounted to the front bumper completes this unit of the Oakbrook Terrace, Illinois, Fire Protection District. (Dennis J. Maag)

Although John Bean was known for its work with water fog systems, it built a long line of other apparatus. This 1963 International Harvester/John Bean had a 750 GPM pump and 250-gallon tank in addition to its 75-foot mid-mount aerial. The red and white rig belonged to the Batesville, Indiana, Fire Department. Such combination rigs proved sufficient for departments of smaller communities. (Steve Hagy)

Although Mack made its own aerial ladders, customer specifications often called for Pirsch aluminum aerials. Elm Grove, Wisconsin, operated this 1965 Mack C95 with a Pirsch mid-ship mounted 85-foot aerial. The truck's Waterous pump was rated at 1,000 GPM. Stainless steel panels surround the lower portion of the cab, and a chrome bell is mounted to the bumper. The Stokes basket attached to the aerial ladder was a common fixture on ladder trucks. (Chuck Madderom)

The fire department of Lake Havasu City, Arizona, purchased this mid-ship mounted aerial ladder from Tempe, Arizona. The 1964 unit was built by Howe, using an International VCO-190 chassis and 85-foot Grove aerial ladder. Grove ladder units are easily identified by their large bed ladder section. Floodlights are mounted atop the rear cabinets, and breathing apparatus is kept in protective covers on the truck's sides. (Garry Kadzielawski)

Open cab trucks, such as this 1968 Crown/Snorkel, were common on the west coast. Snorkel 1 was the pride of the Pacific Grove Fire Department of California's Monterey County. The finish of this truck was the darkest of the variety of reds used for fire apparatus. (Shaun P. Ryan)

White-painted wheels, cab roof, and reflective striping accent this 1968 Crown tractor-drawn aerial of Berkeley, California. Late in the decade, most tractor-drawn aerials were built with four-section aerials that allowed a fixed tiller position. The chassis configuration of tractor-drawn aerial apparatus normally was decided upon by the purchaser and dependent upon options made available by manufacturers. In this case, ground ladder racks were built into the trailer's sides, and the tractor chassis was long enough to accommodate a large cabitnet. White trim was used effectively throughout the livery. (Shaun P. Ryan)

Although Maxim aerials were marketed primarily in the northeast, the firm expanded its apparatus sales during the 1960s as evidenced by this 1964 100-foot F Model for Seattle's Truck 7. Two newer rotating becons augmented the orignial single type on the cab roof. (Bill Hattersley)

Crown specially built this low cab unit to fit in the quarters of Ladder 1 of the Wenatchee, Washington, Fire Department. The 1968 Firecoach featured an 85-foot Snorkel and 1,500 GPM pump. A heightened rear cab, which allowed firefighters to stand, was possible on this rig in view of the boom's stowed height. Tandem axles were common on trucks with booms of 85 feet. (Bill Hattersley)

Seattle ran this massive 1969 Kenworth/Curtis Heiser tractor-drawn 100-foot Maxim aerial as Ladder 1. This was one of two built, with the other going to Ladder 10. Included among their many features were sliding door tiller cabs and ample cabinet space. Kenworth tractors proved themselves solid performers in any climate. The general appearance of this rig reflects the care given apparatus by firefighters. (Bill Hattersley)

Ladder 18 of the Yakima, Washington, Fire Department was this 1968 Seagrave/Western States with 85-foot Hi-Ranger tower. Hi-Ranger units were easily identified by their open lattice articulating booms with cable wheels. The stretch of this lime-yellow body allowed ample space for cabinets and storage of long extension ladders. (Bill Hattersley)

City service trucks had all but disappeared during the 1960s. This rare example, a 1966 American LaFrance 900 Series, served the Kennewick, Washington, Fire Department throughout the decade. (Bill Hattersley)

This 1967 American LaFrance 900 Series protected Longview, Washington. Next to its 100-foot aerial is a hose to quickly put a water tower into operations, and a stokes litter basket. Although outriggers for stability are mounted beneath the ladder turntable, midship mount aerial ladders are considered as having a lesser degree of stability than tractor-drawn rigs, since the latter can be jackknifed. A mid-mount aerial is considered most stable when the aerial is raised and extended over the cab. (Bill Hattersley)

The Seagrave Corporation provided removable protective covers for its open cab apparatus. This 1966 model with 100-foot aerial featured a chrome radiator shell and squared fenders. A Hall-Scott engine powered this truck of the Everett, Washington, Fire Department. (Bill Hattersley)

Chehalis, Washington, operated this rare 1961 Westland "Fireliner" with 85-foot Trump Snorkel. Only five Fireliners are known to have been built from 1960 to 1962. Chehalis also ran a Fireliner pumper. This rig originally was painted overall white. It went to the former Soviet republic of Georgia in 1996. The simple design of Westland's cab kept its cost to a minimum. (Bill Hattersley)

1970s

Unquestionably, the most notable change in fire apparatus during the 1970s was the color switch from traditional red to lime green, also called lime yellow. Not everyone saw the color change as an improvement. Ward LaFrance first offered the color, and competitors followed suit. Sales of lime-green apparatus were good, but near the end of the decade, departments reverted to red, convinced that warning lights were the key to high visibility.

To keep up with competition and demands of the fire service for increased load capacities of unsupported aerial ladders, builders had to redesign aerials for greater strength. The decade also saw changes in trends, such as an increase in orders for diesel-powered apparatus, custom built apparatus, and hydraulic stabilizers. Scene lighting grew more important and the common single six-volt light mounted to truck cabs was replaced by searchlights and light towers.

The 1970 introduction of the Telesqurt, a telescoping combination waterway and ladder, marked the beginning of doing more with less. That especially became evident as urban fire departments began reducing the number of firefighters assigned to fire companies. During the decade, American LaFrance introduced four new models: its 1000 Series in 1971, Pioneer II in 1972, Century in 1973, and Pioneer III in 1976. Manufacture of the company's line of Aero Chief platforms came to an end in 1974. Since 1963, a total of 171 Aero Chiefs had been built in boom heights of 70, 80, and 90 feet. Only five had been built with commercial cabs. Many were quints and some featured tandem rear axles. The only multiple Aero Chief deliveries were to San Diego, which acquired four, and Pittsburgh, which purchased two; four were exported. San Diego, eventually, converted its Aero Chiefs to pumpers.

The decade also signaled the beginning of the quest for larger fire apparatus. Tucson, Arizona, for example, in 1972 purchased its first 150-foot elevating platform, a Calavar Firebird, the tallest aerial in the U.S. Ladder Towers, Inc., better known as LTI, opened its doors in 1973 when it purchased the aerial division of Grove Manufacturing of Shady Grove, Pennsylvania. Soon, LTI joined the competition by turning out various lengths of aerial ladders and platforms.

The Fullerton Fire Department of Orange County, California, operates six stations with as many engine companies, and a single truck company. This American LaFrance Century Series tractor-drawn 100-foot aerial served as Truck 1 until it was replaced and put in reserve. A large hydraulic outrigger extended out and downward from beneath the turntable, while a smaller stabilizer lowered immediately behind the tractor's rear wheels. (Mario and Trina Silva)

Ladder 15 of the Boston Fire Department was a 1976 Seagrave 100-foot tractor trailer unit with four-door cab. This rig was assigned as Ladder 15 until 1989 when it was placed in reserve status. (Scott LaPrade)

Chicago's Truck Co. 55 was this 1973 American LaFrance Century Series with rear-mount 100-foot aerial. Ground ladders were stored horizontally in double banks. The inboard lamps of the truck's bezel headlights reflect Chicago's traditional red and green lights, patterned after those required on vessels. Throughout much of its history, the Chicago Fire Department was a regular customer of American LaFrance. The major drawback to this design was the difficulty and hazard of removing the large extension ladders from their high positioned racks. (Author's Collection)

Baytown, Texas ran this 1977 Ward LaFrance Ambassador with a Hahn four-section, 106-foot "FireSpire" aerial. The FireSpire was more common as a rear-mount than tractor-drawn. Hydraulic A-frame stabilizers supported the truck during aerial operations. Fire axes, a battering ram, and pry tool are mounted to the truck's exterior, a practice that was soon done away with. (Dave Organ)

Truck 12 of the Washington, D.C. Fire Department operated this 1979 American LaFrance Century Series tractor-drawn 100-foot aerial. The Washington, D.C., area is credited with introducing reflective striping during the 1970s. Eventually, the striping would become a requirement for fire apparatus. The four-section aerial allowed a fixed tiller position. (Author's Collection)

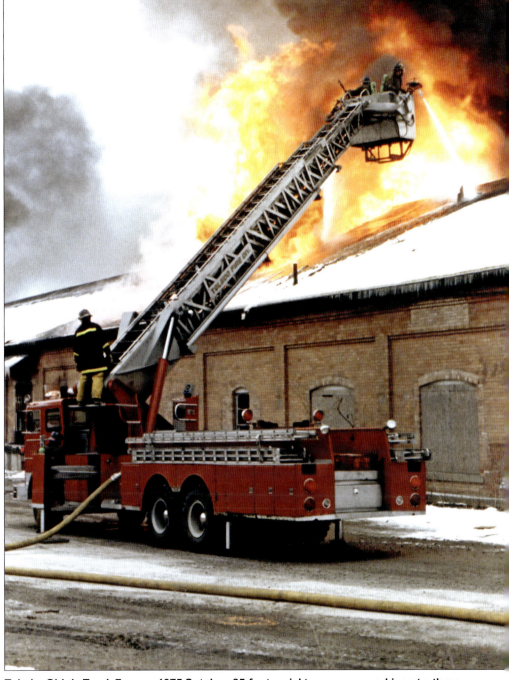

Toledo, Ohio's Truck 7 was a 1975 Sutphen 85-foot aerial tower seen working at a three-alarm warehouse fire. Horizontally extended outriggers beneath the turntable fully stabilize the rig, while vertical stabilizers are lowered behind the dual rear wheels. (Steve Hagy)

New York's Ladder Company 173, which was established in Queens in December 1966, captured the patriotic Bicentennial spirit with this 900 Series American LaFrance. The Wording on the bumper reads, "Spirit of America." Although tractor-drawn aerials were common in the FDNY during the 1970s, their numbers began to diminish in favor of tower ladders and rear-mount aerials. Regardless of the type, all the trucks would be adorned with company artwork. (Author's Collection)

Tractor-drawn aerials by Ward LaFrance were uncommon. Truck 55 of Alexandria, Virginia used a 1978 diesel-powered Ward LaFrance to pull a 100-foot Maxim aerial. The Ward LaFrance firm was noted not only for its liberal use of glass and stainless steel on cabs, but also for its use of the color lime-yellow. The color, also called "lime-green" created a storm of controversy, with traditionalists standing firm on red fire trucks. (Chuck Madderom)

Ward LaFrance called this Ambassador Series chassis with 75-foot Hi-Ranger elevating platform its Senator Series. This 1976 unit served Bridgeport, Connecticut. Since the department ran truck companies with five or six firefighters, the city installed side-facing seats behind the cab, which exposed firefighters to the elements and thrown objects. Trucks retained the unsound seating arrangement until the early 1990s. Hydraulic swing-down stabilizers were in four positions on the truck body. (Lou Tibor)

Snorkel Squads, which provided manpower and equipment at large fires, were placed in service by the Chicago Fire Department beginning with Snorkel Squad 1 in 1962. By 1982, the department had six squad companies covering the city, plus O'Hare International Airport. Squad 5 was built by 3D Metals on a 1975 Hendrickson chassis with 55-foot Snorkel. Besides manpower, all equipment was kept in closed compartments. The 55-foot boom was a standard for Chicago's squads. (Garry E. Kadsielawski)

The FDNY has been Seagrave's biggest customer since 1917. During the 1970s, Seagrave aerial ladder trucks began appearing in large numbers, along with Mack and American LaFrance aerials. Usually, the area to which the truck was assigned dictated the type of apparatus. This early 1970s Seagrave 100-foot rear-mount ran as Ladder 8 in Manhattan. Like a number of FDNY rigs during that period, it was adorned with Bicentennial markings, which included hundreds of stars. (Author's Collection)

The City of Sacramento, California, acquired four Calavar "Firebirds," two purchased new and two purchased second-hand. This 1972 FWD/Calavar 150-footer originally was owned by the Tucson, Arizona, Fire Department in red and white livery. Firebirds, though unpopular with firefighters, were favored by the city council. (Chuck Madderom)

Pierce built this 1974 F Series Ford with 45-foot "Aerial-ett," and 750 GPM pump and 500-gallon water tank. The unique 45-foot Aerial-ett was the product of Halline Utility Company of St. Louis, which specialized in utility-type equipment. Truck 40 of the Waukarusa, Indiana Fire Department also carried 15 gallons of foam. (Garry E. Kadzielawski)

The fire department of Casper, Wyoming replaced a 1954 Seagrave 85-foot aerial with this 1977 Hendrickson/Calavar Firebird 90. The Calavar Corporation of Santa Fe Springs, California, built Firebirds in 90, 125, and 150-foot models. The Model 150 could reach 15 stories in height, 78 feet horizontally, and carry a 1,000-pound load in its platform. (Bill Hattersley)

This 1974 Seagrave tractor-drawn 100-foot aerial of the Baltimore City Fire Department starred in the 2004 film release "Ladder 49." (John A. Calderone/Fire Apparatus Journal)

Built by Pierce, this multi-function apparatus belonged to the Goodwill Fire Company of York Township, Spry, Pennsylvania. Mounted atop the 1975 International Harvester was a 50-foot Tele-Squrt. Besides a pump rated at 1,000 GPM, the rig featured a 500-gallon water tank. (Author's Collection)

When ATO, Inc., the parent company of American LaFrance, purchased Snorkel Fire Equipment Company in 1973, the Aero Chief line was discontinued and orders for elevating platforms became Snorkels. The last four Aero Chiefs were delivered during 1974. The last of these was this American LaFrance Series 1000 Aero chief 80, which was the third for Shreveport, Louisiana. The reverse of this rig's overall colors and reflective striping was considered even more high visibility than red, which was said to appear as black under certain night conditions. (Dave Organ)

Tower 314 of the South Lynches Fire Department, Lake City, South Carolina, was the first Aerialscope built with a pump, requiring tandem rear axles to handle the extra weight. The unit's telescoping boom reached a working height of 75-feet and its pump was rated at 1,500 GPM. It began service with West Trenton, New Jersey, and South Lynches eventually sold it to Clarendon County, South Carolina. Even dark colored reflective striping proved highly visible at night. (Dave Organ)

Although built in 1972, "Platform 2," a 70-foot "Astro Tower" of the Greenville, South Carolina, Fire Department traces its origin back to 1951 when Ted Trump invented the "Giraffe," which was the first truck-mounted articulating platform. The Giraffe was modified to become Chicago's first Snorkel in 1958. Then, in 1972, Seagrave joined with Trump Limited of Oliver, British Columbia, to produce the Astro Tower. Plans existed for an 85-foot unit, but only 70-foot units were built. The term "snorkel," although associated with water, was coined for the unique fire apparatus in Chicago when observers noted that it often operated under massive water streams. (Dave Organ)

American Fire Apparatus built this unit on a 1976 Hendrickson Model 1871S. Topping the rig is an "Aqua Jet," which was American's answer to Snorkel's Tele-Squirt. The pre-piped waterway was rated at 1,000 GPM and was available in 55- and 75-foot lengths. It is estimated that less than 25 Aqua Jets were built between 1972 and 1978. Hendrickson began building fire apparatus during the 1930s, with most having a box-like appearance by the 1970s. The firm introduced the first tandem axle suspension, and was one of the first to use diesel engines. The North Hampton Volunteer Fire Department of Allison Park, Pennsylvania, used this yellow over blue scheme. (Dave Organ)

Ladder 1 of Hopedale, Massachusetts, was a 1973 Maxim with 100-foot mid-mount aerial. In its day, Maxim made ample use of chrome for its radiator grille design. It became a trademark, along with a large windshield, wide engine hood, and squared fenders. Grillework designs on the sides of engine cowls, which hinged open to help cool engines that ran for long periods at fires, often identified a particular manufacturer. Throughout the development of aerial apparatus, all available trailer space was utilized for equipment storage. Such utilization is evident in Ladder1's design. (Dick Bartlett)

In 1976, Young Fire Equipment delivered this rig, called the "King Cobra," to Cherry Hill, New Jersey. It was the first Simon Snorkel unit in the U.S. and one of only two built by Young. Known for building unique features, Young used a low-profile 1976 Hendrickson cab and top-mounted pump panel. The Snorkel had two long booms and a short boom, which allowed the basket to be lowered over parapet walls. Its pre-piped waterway was capable of 1,000 GPM, and the escape ladder ran alongside all three boom sections. The King Cobra ended up with the Forsyth, Georgia Fire Department. (Dave Organ)

Some major corporations equipped their industrial fire departments with fire apparatus that was on a par with those of major cities. Such was the case with Amoco Oil Co., which purchased this 1978 Pierce/Hendrickson for its Whiting, Indiana Refinery. The 75-foot Snorkel unit had a pump rated at 1,250 GPM and carried 744 gallons of foam. In some cases, corporate-owned and operated rigs carried specialized equipment that was tailored to the corporation's manufacturing process. Foam, for example, was commonly required for manufacturing. (Garry E. Kadzielawski)

Daly City, California, ran this 1971 Duplex/Van Pelt with 80-foot Hi-Ranger Snorkel. The open lattice work of Hi-Ranger aerial units made it easier to inspect for wear and damage. Such required safety checks are made by fire departments on a scheduled basis, or if the unit was subjected to extreme temperatures and other stresses. Open cab rigs were a common sight in California's mild climate. (Garry E. Kadzielawski)

Chicago's Truck 14 used this 1975 International to pull a trailer with a 1976 Seagrave 100-foot aerial. The trailer was rebuilt from a 1954 FWD with wooden aerial, a common truck on the CFD. Unusual is the cab's long, vertical exhaust stack. (Garry E. Kadzielawski)

Ward LaFrance offered a variety of aerial devices, including this Teleboom, which it marketed in 1972. Similar to Mack and Sutphen's towers, the Teleboom was built by Reading Techmatic in 75- and 85-foot sizes. Since the Ward LaFrance/Reading devices used the "Tele" prefix, Snorkel filed suit and the names of the devices were changed. Reading Techmatic separated from Ward LaFrance and sold Telebooms to other makers, including Boardman, which purchased Reading Techmatic in 1983. After a nationwide tour, the first Teleboom, a 75-foot unit built on a 1973 Ford, was sold to Fox Lake, Illinois, who later sold it to Comer, Georgia. The bulky unit incorporated a 1,000 GPM pump and 750-gallon water tank, requiring a tandem rear axle. (Garry E. Kadzielawski)

The Lisle-Woodridge Fire Protection District of Illinois ran this 1974 Pirsch 100-foot rear-mount aerial, which was rebuilt by Pierce in 1984. Its pump was rated at 1,250 GPM. (Garry E. Kadzielawski)

This attractive 75-foot Snorkel unit of Munster, Indiana, was built by Pierce on a 1971 Maxim chassis. A 200-gallon water tank augmented its 1,000 GPM pump. (Garry E. Kadzielawski)

Ladder 3 of Sturgis, Michigan used an 85-foot Canadian-built Pierre Thibault aerial on a 1977 Mack CF Model. Hamerly, which built the rig, later added a 1,000 GPM pump with control panel to the front of the cab. (Garry E. Kadzielawski)

The Griffith, Indiana, Fire Department built this rig using an ex-Gary, Indiana, rebuilt 1970 American LaFrance 900 Series chassis, and a 1948 70-foot Maxim aerial formerly used by Whiting, Indiana. It was aptly named the "Water Chief," having a 1,500 GPM pump and 1,200-gallon water tank. A diamond-tread staircase was necessary to access the aerial turntable. (Garry E. Kadzielawski)

Van Pelt built this 6x6 Fabco unit on a 1971 International with 85-foot Grove aerial for Mammoth Lakes, California. Features of the heavy duty truck included a 750 GPM pump and IHC V-8 gasoline engine. The high position of the cab required a boarding step, and that the fender have a sculpted side panel. (Garry E. Kadzielawski)

Van Pelt built this tough truck using a 1977 International Paystar F-5000 and 75-foot LTI aerial. Truck 923 of the Truckee, California, Fire District also featured a 1,250 GPM pump and 500-gallon water tank. Drop-down stabilizers for the aerial were located behind the rear wheels. (Garry E. Kadzielawski)

Union Fire & Rescue of Wheeler, Indiana purchased this brutish rig from the Bethlehem Steel Corporation. Powered by a Caterpillar diesel engine, Tower 1228 was rebuilt by Fire Apparatus Services using a 1973 Ford C8000 and 75-foot Sutphen tower ladder. A 1,000 GPM pump and 300-gallon water tank completed the unit. Tower ladders were built to maximize the effectiveness fo both aerial ladders and buckets found on snorkel booms. (Garry E. Kadzielawski)

After refurbishment by Kenco, this 1977 American LaFrance mid-mount 100-foot Century Series aerial truck bears little resemblance to its original state. The busy face of the cab includes two sets of bezel lights, along with a dated Roto-Ray light. Truck 159 belonged to the Clymer Fire Company of Indiana County, Pennsylvania. The various colors and their disruptive pattern on this truck ensured its high visibility as much as a truck painted a single color. Liberal use of chrome also aided in reflecting light. (Patrick Shoop, Jr.)

Moon Township of Alleghany County, Pennsylvania, operated this 1972 Oshkosh/Pierce unit with 85-foot Snorkel and 1,250 GPM pump. Truck 197's distinctive blue and white livery was enhanced by white reflective striping. Pierce Manufacturing relied heavily upon Cincinnati cabs for its fire apparatus. The cab's simple design proved highly functional in affording spaciousness and good visibility. (Patrick Shoop, Jr.)

Chicago made wide use of commercial Ford cabs, including this 1970 C8000 built by Pierce with 55-foot Snorkel and 1,000 GPM pump. This rig served as Chicago's Snorkel 3 and 6. (Author's Collection)

It was not unusual for fire departments, when ordering new apparatus, to specify its dimensions, thereby avoiding costly station remodeling. Conestoga, which was a division of LTI, built this low profile Oshkosh/Van Pelt cab with 100-foot LTI aerial for Oceanside, California, in 1978. A 370 h.p. Detroit diesel engine powered the unit. (Chuck Madderom)

The Chicago Fire Department's search for an aerial with the farthest reach for its high-rise district led to this unique unit. Pierce constructed the truck by mating a Japanese 135-foot, six-section Morita Lift to a Hendrickson chassis. The special aerial was delivered in 1974 and assigned to Hook & Ladder 1. (Author's Collection)

Truck 8 of Oakland, California, used this 1973 Seagrave tractor-drawn 100-foot aerial, powered by a 350-h.p. diesel engine. West Coast fire departments continued to use wooden ground ladders long after most cities had switched to aluminum. A big advantage over metal ladders was wood's inability to conduct electricity. (Chuck Madderom)

Three builders had a hand in completing this truck for the Springfield, Oregon, Fire Department in 1972. Pierce built the unit using a Crown cab and 85-foot Snorkel. Its pump was rated at 1,250 GPM. Unusual is the fold-down platform to access the pump panel and quick-attack hose lines. (Bill Hattersley)

The Chelan County Fire District of Sunnyslope, Washington, used this 1977 American quint with 1,500 GPM pump and 65-foot Aqua-Jet. The pipe boom, along with its attached aerial, and ground ladders made this a top-heavy rig. (Bill Hattersley)

Truck 3 of Cary, North Carolina, is a city service truck built by Alexander Body Company on a 1975 GMC L-6500 chassis. Cary is a suburb of Raleigh and has operated several city service trucks, some into the 21st Century. Besides a full complement of ground ladders and truck company tools, city service trucks commonly carried generators and lighting equipment. (Dave Organ)

Wrecked during rail delivery to the SeaTac, Washington, Fire Department, this 1970 American LaFrance 900 Series with 100-foot aerial was rebuilt by the department. A Cincinnati cab was used to resemble a Mack C125 pumper then in service with the department. (Bill Hattersley)

A 1974 Crown with 1,250 GPM pump and 100-foot Maxim aerial for Salt Lake County, Utah. Gold scrollwork and trim, which was reminiscent of a bygone era, was applied throughout the rig. (Bill Hattersley)

This Mack CF tower ladder served Darien, Connecticut, in the 1970s. With all six of its stabilizers down, the truck's front wheels are off the ground, giving the platform all-around stability. The tower could then be fully rotated and extended. No single type of fire apparatus better displayed the advantage of hydraulics than the Aerialscope. (Lou Tibor)

Mack ladder trucks bearing Maxim aerial ladders were a common combination. This 1975 Mack CF wore a Maxim 85-foot aerial for duty with the U.S. Marine Corps at Quantico, Virginia. Mack's CF fire model enjoyed a 24-year production run of more than 3,800 vehicles, beginning in 1967. The CF cab was praised for its roominess and excellent visibility. Like municipal fire departments, the military bid on apparatus from various makers. Mack's longevity and popularity made it an easy choice. (Shaun P. Ryan)

The Yuma, Arizona, Fire Department operated this 1976 Maxim with 100-foot mid-mount aerial from 1977 to 1995. It was then sold to Brawley, California. Mid-mount aerials proved very stable due to their position on the chassis, especially in combination with stabilizers. (Bill Hattersley)

Kenworth was a popular make of truck with the Seattle Fire Department, and with other northwest departments. Curtis/Heiser specialized in building fire apparatus onto Kenworth chassis. One example was Seattle's Ladder 11, which was one of three 1972 units built with 100-foot Maxim aerials. Stabilizing jacks stored in recessed areas beneath turntables were a common fixture on ladder trucks during the 1970s. Due to the cab's immense size, vertical guide poles were attached to the front bumper corners to help the driver estimate the position of the cab's outside corners. (Bill Hattersley)

Although Pirsch cab-forward tractors were popular, the firm continued its line of engine-forward tractors. The square fender style first appeared in 1955. The Bloomington, Minnesota, Fire Department ran this 1972 100-foot Senior aerial truck with five-person cab. Road sander units were mounted to the fenders covering the tractor's dual wheels. This rig carried a total of 240 feet of ground ladders, which ranged from 12 to 55 feet. (Author's Collection)

Milwaukee was a loyal customer of Mack and Pirsch, and the "McPirsch" aerial remained popular into the 1970s. Ladder Company 2's "Big Stick" was a 1972 diesel-powered, 100-foot unit that protected the downtown area. During the decade, Milwaukee employed a mix of tractor-drawn, rear-mount, and mid-mount aerial ladders. All ladder companies were then staffed by a crew of five. (Gerrit Madderom)

Milwaukee's Ladder Company 13 used this unusual Mack-Pirsch combination. In 1978, the department shop rebuilt a 1956 Pirsch 85-foot aerial ladder trailer, and mated it with a diesel-powered Mack MB custom canopy cab tractor. Only 319 MB custom fire units were built from 1972 to 1978. Screw-down stabilizing jacks were tucked below the turntable. A generator and smoke fan are secured to the running board. (Gerrit Madderom)

Truck 6 of the Newark, New Jersey Fire Department was a Mack CF with Snorkel, which was housed with Engine 13. Newark switched from red to lime-yellow with white cab roofs for its fire apparatus during the early 1970s. The upper boom of Truck 6's Snorkel unit is accented with a gold stripe. Since the folded booms extended beyond the cab, a warning light and siren were mounted to each side of the cab roof. Boom buckets were wrapped with fire resistive material to protect firefighters from flames and icy winds. (Author's Collection)

This American LaFrance experimental ladder platform made its debut in 1970. This was a demonstrator only and the type never went into production. The Nixon-Egli Equipment Company, which specializes in construction vehicles, was instrumental in the unit's design and fabrication. The cab of the massive rig wears the emblem of ATO, a corporate giant, which became the parent company of American LaFrance in 1966. Four hydraulically-operated vertical stabilizers ensured a stable platform. (Author's Collection)

1980s

As municipal budgets became tighter, and the cost of new apparatus increased markedly during the decade, the appeal of refurbishing older fire apparatus reached new heights. In most cases, even completely rebuilding a truck was a significant saving over purchasing a new vehicle. Fire departments often did the work in their shops or turned to local metal fabricating or automotive businesses to complete the job. Refurbishment of older vehicles wasn't limited to pumpers and aerials since specialized vehicles were appearing in large numbers across the country, in both urban and suburban communities. Budget constraints also encouraged widespread use of multi-function apparatus. The best example of that is the St. Louis Fire Department, which at one time operated 26 hook and ladders. That number was reduced to 16 during the 1970s, and was further reduced to ten when a new concept was implemented. In view of the city's decline in population and distressed economy, the decision was made to replace the fleet of pumpers with quints. This "Total Quint Concept" also called for only four hook and ladder companies, three of which were new 110-foot aerials. In late 2009, St. Louis officials decided to assign a hook and ladder unit to each of six districts, still a significantly smaller number of ladder trucks than other major cities.

Quickly fading were the days of riding the tailboard as greater concern for safety resulted in larger, enclosed cabs that accommodate firefighters. Although open cabs were less common, some builders received orders for them until the early 1980s. Roll-up compartment doors, which had long been popular on European fire apparatus, began to appear on American vehicles. Rear-mount aerials grew in popularity during the 1980s. In 1981, Mack Trucks signed an agreement that LTI would build four-section, 106-foot steel rear-mount aerials for Mack's "Bulldog 1." Only 25 were built before Mack quit making fire apparatus in 1983.

A view of the corporate level gave rise to the adage that only the strong survive. Some apparatus firms expanded, while others dropped by the wayside. Pirsch finally closed its doors in 1986, having been the oldest privately owned corporation in Wisconsin. After foundering, Maxim shut down in 1980, re-opened under new ownership in 1985, but ceased operations at the end of the decade. Pierce, meanwhile, along with Emergency One (E-One), expanded.

Many fire departments in the Chicago area adopted the Windy City's color scheme, as seen on this 1980 Pirsch 100-foot aerial of Evergreen Park. (Garry E. Kadzielawski)

Emergency One, better known as E-One, introduced its "Hurricane" series of fire apparatus in 1983. Chicago was a regular E-One customer, with Truck Co. 2's 1988 110-foot aerial among a large number of orders. Truck 2 was stationed with Engine 5 and protected Chicago's downtown area. (Author's Collection)

Denver's Truck 9 was a 1984 Seagrave 100-foot rear-mount aerial, which was rebuilt in 1994. The Denver Fire Department has a long tradition of overall white apparatus, although with frequent changes of markings. A placard affixed to the aerial reads, "STARTRUCK IX First and Foremost in Auto Extrication." Despite Denver's experiments with a number of apparatus markings, the department retained the overall white scheme. (Patrick Campbell)

Steeldraulics Products, Inc. (SPI) only built two tractor-drawn aerial ladder trucks, and both served the San Francisco Fire Department, as Trucks 1 and 13. The massive Cummins diesel-powered units were built on 1986 Spartan Gladiator chassis with 100-foot aerials. The rigs were plagued with too many problems, including poor visibility for the tiller driver, and both were out of service by the end of 1988. (Chuck Madderom)

Another pair of SPI trucks purchased by San Francisco also proved troublesome. Also built on 1986 Spartan Gladiator chassis, these units featured 1,500 GPM pumps and 75-foot aerial ladders, and were earmarked for Engine Companies 20 and 43. They were found to have construction problems and difficulty in negotiating some streets, so they were not placed in service, but were sold in 1988 to Marysville, California, and Branson, Missouri. (Chuck Madderom)

A portion of the Total Quint Concept implemented by the City of St. Louis during the late 1980s involved the purchase of three 1988 Spartan Monarch trucks with 1989 LTI 110-foot aerial ladders. The fourth hook and ladder was a 1981 Sutphen tower, which was the department's first quint. This is Hook & Ladder 15, which was replaced in 2009 by a 125-foot Spartan Evolution Gladiator built by Smeal. All St. Louis fire companies operate with a crew of four. (Mark Stampfl)

Although the apparatus of St. Louis Fire Department Hook & Ladder No. 40 was identical to the city's other truck companies, it was painted in keeping with the practice of lime-yellow for apparatus assigned to airports. This 1989 Spartan with 110-foot LTI aerial ladder features a 1,250 GPM pump, 250-gallon water tank, and 20 gallons of foam. (Garry E. Kadzielawski)

Emergency-One opened its doors in 1974 as an ambulance builder, and five years later produced its first aerial device. The Florida firm became a leader in welded aluminum aerial ladders, even building its own aluminum cabs and chassis. The sections of its different size aerials were interchangeable, with a 135-foot ladder reigning as the tallest built in the U.S. Washington, D.C.'s Truck 6 was the second of five ordered on E-One's popular Hurricane chassis. This 1989, five-section 135-foot "StratoSpear" had an unusual seat enclosure added to the rear of the cab. Truck 6 is housed with Engine 11 in the "House of Flame." (Dave Organ)

After Boardman purchased the Tele-boom design in 1983, the firm built this one-of-a-kind rear-mount unit with a 1981 Hendrickson Model 1871 WS chassis; all others were mid-mount. The 85-foot Tele-boom originally went to South trail, Florida, before being sold to Newberry, South Carolina, to equip Tower 1. The truck's pump was rated at 1,500 GPM. (Dave Organ)

After rebuild by a local truck body shop in 1987, this 1972 Mack/Pirsch of the Milwaukee Fire Department received a four-door crew cab, enclosed tiller, and new cabinets with roll-up doors. Assigned to Ladder Co. No. 17, the Mack CF was diesel-powered and featured a 100-foot aluminum aerial. (Mark Hoeller)

Like its famed family of aircraft, Grumman gave its line of custom and commercial fire apparatus feline names. After Grumman Allied Industries acquired Howe Fire Apparatus in 1976, its Emergency Products Division in Roanoke, Virginia, became a large and well known builder of fire apparatus. When it ceased operations in 1992, M&W Fire Apparatus took over the line. Broadview, Illinois operated this 1989 quint built by Grumman on a 1985 American LaFrance century chassis. Besides its 102-foot "Aerial Cat" platform, the truck featured a 2,000 GPM pump and 300-gallon water tank. Located near the base of the aerial is a breathing air container and quartz floodlights. Grumman's aerial ladders are easily identified by their heavy construction. (Garry E. Kadzielawski)

Wearing a cream and white color scheme, this 75-foot Snorkel unit was built on a 1985 Spartan by Van Pelt/GMC. Powered by a Cummins NTC-400 diesel engine, the truck features a 1,500 GPM pump and 300-gallon water tank. (Garry E. Kadzielawski)

Large numbers of these Century Series 75-foot "Water Chiefs" were built by American LaFrance. Some had their aerials removed and the rig converted to a triple combination pumper after waterways corroded and the aerials proved difficult to maintain. Tulare, California used this 1980 model with 1,500 GPM Twin-Flow pump and 300-gallon water tank. Adding to this rig's versatility is the hose reel above the pump. The reel contained rubber one-inch diameter hose and could be electrically rewound. Using water from the tank, the reel eliminated the need for fabric hose layouts at small fires. (Chuck Madderom)

Squad companies have long been a fixture of the Chicago Fire Department. Operating as a two-piece unit to form a heavy rescue component manned by six firefighters, the squads provide manpower cross-trained in various functions, and specialized equipment. The aerial component uses a 55-foot Snorkel, often used to reach alleyways and tight spaces that are common in the city. Squad 1 during the 1980s ran with this 1987 Spartan Gladiator built by E-One. Later, metal kick panels were added to the bottom of the cab, and the warning light on the front grille was removed. (Garry E. Kadzielawski)

Ladder 4 of the Detroit, Michigan, Fire Department ran this 1983 American LaFrance Century with 100-foot rear-mount aerial ladder. Contained in the truck body was a 150 GPM pump and 250-gallon water tank for small fires not requiring the response of a pumper. (Garry E. Kadzielawski)

It was not unusual for fire departments to order apparatus designed to fit in existing fire stations. The Forest Park, Illinois, Fire Department purchased this low-profile 1980 Oshkosh/Pierce unit with 100-foot LTI tower and 1,250 GPM pump. Many fire departments in the Chicago area adopted the Windy City's black over red scheme for its fire apparatus. (Dennis J. Maag)

Between 1970 and 1987, Baker Equipment Engineering Co. of Richmond, Virginia, would build 340 75-foot tower ladders on Mack chassis. Most were Mack CF Models, with 155 of the 75-foot Aerialscopes going to the FDNY; the department also purchased 17 95-foot units. Ladder 41's 1987 Aerialscope was built by Saulsbury Fire Rescue of Tully, New York. Housed with Engine 90 in the West Farms area of the Bronx, Ladder 41 is one of New York's busiest ladder companies. (Garry E. Kadzielawski)

Truck 10 of the Grand Chute Fire Department of Appleton, Wisconsin, was a 1983 Hendrickson built by 3D Metals with a Canadian-built 100-foot Thibault aerial ladder and 1,250 GPM pump. Hendrickson Mobile Equipment, Inc. of Wyoming, Michigan, became simply HME during the 1980s to reflect its diverse line of equipment. The decade signaled the beginning of the addition of equipment to the tip of the aerial's fly section. (Garry E. Kadzielawski)

The Honolulu, Hawaii, Fire Department ran this 1981 Seagrave with 100-foot, four-section rear-mount aerial from its Kapolei Station. Honolulu, known for its large apparatus to conduct multiple operations, has long relied upon this overall chrome yellow scheme. Station assignments displayed on cab doors are a standard marking. Tandem rear axles became more common as truck weight increased. (Shaun P. Ryan)

Grumman built this unit on a 1988 Duplex chassis to handle any emergency at Sacramento, California's International Airport. Rescue 2 had a 1,250 GPM pump, 1,500 gallons of water, 210 gallons of AFFF, and 200 pounds of Halon, and was topped with a 55-foot Snorkel. Such vehicles could be used for both aircraft emergencies and structure fires. (Garry E. Kadzielawski)

Following service with the Porterville, California, Fire Department, this 1983 Duplex/Van Pelt was acquired by the Lindsay Fire Department. The aerial is a 75-foot LTI, while the pump is a 1,500 GPM Hale with 300-gallon water tank. The color yellow in various shades made inroads to the fire service during the 1980s, with white a common color for aerial ladders. (Chuck Madderom)

Everett, Washington, ran this sturdy 1984 Hendrickson as Ladder 5. The tandem axle rig featured a 1,500 GPM pump, 500-gallon water tank, and 65-foot Thibault mid-mount aerial. Although mounting a 65-foot aerial ladder, this heavy duty rig required tandem rear axles. Hendricksons became well known for their boxy appearing cabs. (Bill Hattersley)

Seattle's Ladders 9 and 11 operated 1980 Ward LaFrance/Curtis-Heiser trucks with Maxim rear-mount 100-foot aerials. Ward LaFrance introduced the dual angle windshield two decades before this rig was built. The unique design offered superior visibility to the driver. Broad stainless steel panels surrounded the roomy cab, and the siren was incorporated into an abbreviated grille. (Bill Hattersley)

Chicago's Truck 32 was among a number of aerials originally mounted on 1966 Mack Chassis, and slated for updating with 1985 Ford C-8000 chassis. Although Pirsch ceased operations in 1986, new, but short-term, owners completed the work in 1988. The trucks featured rebuilt aerial ladders, rehabbed body work, and an enclosed rear cab for firefighters. Truck 32 was housed with Engine 109. (Gerrit Madderom)

Van Pelt built five of these units on Crown Firecoach chassis. This rare 1984 combination ran as Truck E-3S of the Lakeside, California, Fire Department. Its pump was rated at 1,500 GPN and it carried 500 gallons of water. Typical of the Tele-Squrt, its 50 foot-unit combined a pre-piped waterway boom with aerial ladder. (Bill Hattersley)

American LaFrance normally built its Water Chiefs with pumps. This exception, with 75-foot boom, was built in 1983 for the fire department of Ukiah, California. The absence of a pump permitted a liberal use of cabinets. At the rear of the unit were recessed steps to allow access to the aerial ladder atop the boom. During the decade, aerial ladders changed dramatically in appearance as they became equipped with multi-purpose systems. (Bill Hattersley)

The Santa Clara County Central Fire District of California used this 1981 Duplex/Van Pelt truck with a 55-foot LTI aerial, 1,500 GPM pump, and 500-gallon water tank. (Bill Hattersley)

The craze in aerial waterway boom/ladders continued into the 1980s with LTI's 55-foot "Fire Stix." The steel pipeway topped with aluminum rescue ladder was mounted to this 1982 Spartan/Van Pelt of the Gilroy, California, Fire Department. The Fire Stix gave a short wheelbase rig great maneuverability with an aerial device. In 1987, Kovatch Mobile Equipment, or KME, purchased the Fire Stix from LTI and added a 75-foot version to its line. Like most units, Gilroy's featured a 1,500 GPM pump and 500-gallon water tank. (Bill Hattersley)

After Ladder Towers, Inc., or LTI, acquired Grove's aerial division in 1974, it began turning out successful aerials, both tractor-drawn and single-chassis. Milwaukee ordered this LTI 108-foot aerial ladder pulled by a 1985 Ford LS tractor canopy cab. The tiller position was fully enclosed and featured bulged side windows for added visibility since the aerial hindered the view forward. All cabinets had roll-up doors. Ladder Co. 2 protected Milwaukee's downtown area. (Gerrit Madderom)

With more than 60 truck companies, the Chicago Fire Department is the second largest in the U.S. Since Emergency-One opened its doors in the 1970s, Chicago was a prime customer for its ladder trucks. Truck 30, which runs with Engine 47 in Chicago's Woodlawn area, used this 1982 E-One 110-foot, rear-mount aerial built on a Hendrickson chassis. (Gerrit Madderom)

Everett, Washington, ran this sturdy 1984 Hendrickson as Ladder 5. The tandem axle rig featured a 1,500 GPM pump, 500-gallon water tank, and 65-foot Thibault mid-mount aerial. Although somewhat boxy in appearance, this cab style was Hendrickson's first major deviation from its standard box-shape design. High ladder guardrails not only increased strength, they increased the safety margin for firefighters. (Bill Hattersley)

The Springdale Fire Company of Stratford, Connecticut, ran three pumpers and one truck, which was this 1985 Custom Cab Ford mounting a 65-foot Snorkel unit. Smaller communities found their aerial ladder needs fulfilled with articulating units that were augmented by ground ladders, such as those mounted to the side of Truck 56. Reflective striping was a later addition, which became an NFPA requirement during the next decade. (Lou Tibor)

Mack Trucks' MC Series of custom fire apparatus proved highly successful, with 756 of the type produced between 1978 and 1990. Milwaukee's fondness for the Mack/Pirsch aerial ladder truck ended with this Mack MC with Pirsch 100-foot rear-mount aerial delivered in 1983 and assigned to Ladder Co. 9. (Gary Rudek)

Six sturdy stabilizers allowed Mack's Aerialscope to provide a solid working platform totally independent of the vehicle's suspension. Thanks to the flexibility of the tower ladder, the members of Larchmont, New York's Hook & Ladder Company 1 have excellent coverage of this building, which is fully involved with fire. (Author's Collection)

1990s

The revised standards for fire apparatus issued by the NFPA in 1991 meant new approaches in apparatus design for both industry and fire departments. A significant requirement of the new standard, called NFPA 1901, called for all firefighters to ride in enclosed, seated positions. While NFPA 1901 did not specify apparatus color, it did set standards for reflective striping and warning lights. The decade saw a nearly complete return to traditional red, although usually in combination with white. Stringent standards and federal regulations impacted fire apparatus to the extent that the cost of custom apparatus skyrocketed, leading to even greater use of commercial chassis. The use of multi-function vehicles continued to rise during the 1990s as departments of all sizes struggled with staffing shortages. These conditions brought about a number of changes among fire apparatus builders.

During the decade, some of the big names in fire apparatus production closed their doors. First was Crown Coach in 1991, followed by Van Pelt and Beck in 1992. Mack discontinued its line of custom fire apparatus, and in 1994 American LaFrance stopped fire apparatus production. Freightliner would acquire limited rights to the firm's "Eagle" Series. Boardman closed its doors in 1995, and in 1996 Oshkosh Trucks purchased Pierce so that Oshkosh could be less dependent on military orders.

On 30 December 1991, the Fire Department of New York (FDNY) took delivery of its last Aerialscope built on a Mack chassis. A total of 172 Aerialscopes had served the FDNY since 1964. Although massive aerial platforms of various makes became popular, the time-honored aerial ladder held its own. In the interest of combining operations using multi-function vehicles, aerial ladder-waterway booms became a common sight on pumpers.

In 1990 Seagrave introduced its Apollo aerial platform, which was a bulky unit that reached a height of 105 feet. After its demonstration tour, in 1992 the first unit went to the Denver Fire Department, which painted it in the department livery of overall white. The Apollo had a 1,500 GPM pump and 150-gallon water tank. The yellow cylinder above the hydraulic arm at the aerial's base contained breathing air that was channeled to firefighters operating in the bucket. (Dave Organ)

Painted in the attractive licensed artwork to celebrate Idaho's Centennial in 1990, Pocatello's Engine No. 2 was a 1990 Pierce Arrow with 55-foot aerial and 1,500 GPM pump. (Bill Hattersley)

Smart looking in its white scheme with gold trim, Denver's Truck 23 was a 1996 Spartan Gladiator built by Smeal. The unit used a 75-foot aerial, along with a 1,250 GPM pump and 300-gallon water tank. (Patrick Campbell)

Painted the department's traditional overall white for fire apparatus, Aerial Tower 1 of the New Haven, Connecticut, Fire Department was a 1996 Sutphen aerial platform. (Lou Tibor)

The Walnut Street Fire Company of the Madison, Indiana, Fire Department operated this 1994 Seagrave 100-foot aerial unit, with 1,250 GPM pump and 250-gallon tank. Truck No. 4 wears on its cab doors a cloverleaf with Dutch shoes, complimenting the rig's emerald green color scheme. Shamrocks are commonly seen on fire apparatus not only to channel luck of the Irish and reflect ethnic pride, but to symbolize to the Irish that they were welcomed as fire service employees. Displaying the symbol harks back to the days when Irish and Scottish immigrants were barred from employment other than the tough and dangerous work as firefighters and police officers. (Steve Hagy)

Springfield, Oregon Fire & Life Safety operated this 1998 Pierce Dash 85-foot tower with all-wheel steering. Powered by a Detroit Series 60 500 h.p. diesel engine, the truck featured a 1,500 GPM pump, 500-gallon tank, and 25 gallons of foam. The tower went to Merrill, Wisconsin, which retained the unique color scheme and markings. The emblem on the bucket is reminiscent of those worn during colonial days. (Bill Hattersley)

This 1999 Pierce Quantum with 75-foot aerial was assigned to Honolulu's Kailua Station. The tandem-axle truck is powered by a 470 h.p. Detroit diesel engine and has a 1,500 GPM pump with 500-gallon water tank. During the late 1990s, Honolulu apparatus began appearing with white upper cabs. White reflective striping, along with white aerial equipment made for a highly visible truck. Heavily tinted windows to shield against heat and glare were considered a must. (Chuck Madderom)

Although used in Canada, this unit is believed to be the only one of its kind in the U.S. Built by HME/Boardman with a Canadian-built Nova Quintech aerial, the 1994 truck belonged to the Braddock, Pennsylvania, Volunteer Fire Department 2. Besides its 1,500 GPM pump, the truck mounts Nova Quintech's "Sky-Five" five-section 100-foot aerial ladder. In its retracted state, the ladder is the shortest 100-foot aerial in the fire service, allowing for short vehicle length and greater maneuverability. In 1997, Pierce purchased the Nova Quintech aerial line. Most unusual is the hinged hose reel attached to the side of the aerial. A 50-foot section of 2 ½-inch hose was carried on the reel. (Dan Decher)

Finished in metallic burgundy, Tower 93 of the Columbus, Wisconsin, Fire Department is this 1997 diesel-powered Pierce Lance 100-foot aerial unit with 1,500 GPM pump and 200-gallon water tank. Pierce incorporated narrow stairs at the rear of the body to access the aerial turntable. Since the cardinal bird is a popular theme in Columbus, and the symbol of local school sports teams, a cardinal caricature is worn on the tower's bucket. (Chuck Madderom)

The fire department of Naval Air Station Patuxent River, Maryland, in 1996 took delivery of this KME 102-foot AerialCat on a Renegade low-profile, full-tilt chassis with 1,500 GPM pump. Weighing 32 tons, the unit is powered by a Detroit diesel. The truck's H-style outriggers are extended and lowered. Fire departments of military installations typically patterned their structural fire apparatus after those of municipalities. The aerial ladder unit of this rig is among the largest that a truck can accommodate. (Mike Wilson)

This 1993 Seagrave Patriot with 100-foot aerial ladder belonged to Chicago's Truck 33. This was Chicago's first tilt-cab, rear-mount aerial. Powered by a Detroit diesel engine with Allison transmission, this was one of six such units ordered. Truck 33 runs with Engine 49 to protect Chicago's New City neighborhood. This truck was highly efficient in design with its roomy cab with rear entry door, relatively short wheelbase for maneuverability through city streets, and oversize cabinets for large equipment. Low positioned headlights were found to be more efficient and safer for the driver in preventing glare. On each side of the cab was a sliding window. (Bill Friedrich)

Details of Ladder 7's 1992 Seagrave, including tiller position and surf board, which was standard equipment on Honolulu ladder trucks. Surf boards were used for surf rescue from 6 PM to 9 AM when life guards were off-duty. Cabinets are in abundance on this maximum-size tractor and trailer. (Wayne Jasper-Fire Find)

Spartan's Baron of the 1990s is distinguished by its mid-chassis mounted pump, in the case of this 1990 Baron, a Godiva 1,500 GPM rated unit. The Clark County Fire Department of Laughlin, Nevada, owned this Baron, which had a 100-foot LTI aerial ladder. It was powered by a Detroit 475 h.p. diesel engine. Mounted on he bed ladder of this aerial, immediately behind the hydraulic lift cylinder, is a yellow cylinder containing pressurized breathing air for firefighters working in the bucket. (Chuck Madderom)

Wearing the state caricature of "Bucky Badger" on its bucket, this 1996 Pierce Lance served the fire department of Oconomowoc, Wisconsin. Powered by a Detroit Series 60 470 h.p. diesel engine, the rig featured a 100-foot platform, in addition to a Waterous 1,500 GPM pump and 300-gallon water tank. Mounted on the front bumper is an American LaFrance bell. Tandem rear axles have become standard on platform apparatus. (Chuck Madderom)

Wearing the livery of Clark County, Nevada, this 1992 E-One Hurricane was the first of the firm's 105-foot towers, which was called the HP-105. Its pump was rated at 1,500 GPM and it carried a 150-gallon water tank. The rig was later sold to Tonopah, Nevada. Truck 16, like most towers, had twin master stream nozzles on its bucket. (Chuck Madderom)

Truck 29 of the Los Angeles City Fire Department was a 1996 Simon Duplex with 100-foot LTI aerial ladder. Not unusual for a west coast truck are wooden extension ladders. On its frame, beneath the turntable, is a dedication to a fallen firefighter. (Chuck Madderom)

Columbia, Illinois claimed this unusual 1992 Boardman built on a Ford L8000 chassis with Towers 55-foot Apache tower and 1,000 GPM front-mounted pump. The rig also carried a 500-gallon water tank. (Dennis J. Maag)

Originally placed in service with the North Palos, Illinois, Fire Department, this 1998 HME/3D Metals rig went to Taylorville, Illinois. Tower 804 featured a 100-foot Nova Quintech Skyarm and 1,500 GPM pump and 300-gallon water tank. It seemed that tower units built during the 1990s, such as Taylorville's, couldn't be built any larger. Both truck and aerial were immense, requiring rugged construction, tandem rear axles, and massive powerplants. State of the art warning light systems compensated for the liberal amount of black used in this truck's livery. (Dennis J. Maag)

Washington, D.C.'s Truck 13 was a 1993 Simon Duplex with LTI 100-foot aerial ladder. The capitol department's mix of red and white colors formed one of the most highly visible schemes. Stars were incorporated into the scheme and the official city emblem was displayed on the cab doors. Applying large company numbers to front grilles was a common practice. Besides the cab, a roomy workspace was fabricated for the tiller person, complete with sliding door and bulged side windows to see alongside the truck. (Author's Collection)

Henderson, Nevada's Truck 42 was a 1995 E-One Hurricane with 105-foot HP-105 tower and 1,500 GPM pump. Power was supplied by a Detroit 475 h.p. diesel engine. As much as the lines of the reflective striping have an artistic flair, they are meant to be disruptive to the overall white color, and therefore are eye-catching. The truck's large number of chrome components also enhanced visibility. (Chuck Madderom)

This rig was unique not only in its silver over red color scheme, but that fact that its rescue basket at the end of its 85-foot Aerial Innovations tower ladder was detachable. Built by Quality on a Spartan chassis, this rig operated as Ladder 2 of Iona, Michigan's Department of Public Safety. The sturdy rig also featured a 2,000 GPM pump, 1,000-gallon water tank, and 150 gallons of foam concentrate. (Garry E. Kadzielawski)

Honolulu's Ladder 7 was one of eight Seagrave tractor-trailer 100-foot aerials ordered during the early 1990s. Sationed at Waikiki, Ladder 7 was built with fully enclosed riding positions for its crew. Honolulu's wide streets and mild climate allowed fire department officials to rely upon the largest available tractor-drawn apparatus. (Wayne Jasper-Fire Find)

Aerial 44 of the City La Grande, Oregon, Fire and Rescue typified cost-saving rehabbing that continued into the 1990s. American LaFrance in 2001 combined a 1996 Freightliner with a 1968 80-foot Aero Chief unit. Extending a commercial cab was common and still proved less costly than a custom cab and chassis. It was also common to combine components from differently aged apparatus. (Garry E. Kadzielawski)

Patriotic themes for fire apparatus were in vogue during the 1990s. California's City of Napa used this striking stars and stripes pattern, which aided in high visibility, on its 1994 Duplex with LTI 105-foot aerial. A 1,750 GPM pump provided an ample water supply. The large yellow reel alongside the aerial holds a heavy duty power cord that supplies power to the aerial tip. (Garry E. Kadzielawski)

This attractive, high-visibility rig hailed from the Honolulu, Hawaii, Fire Department, which ran the unit from its Kailua Station. Ladder 19 is a 1999 Pierce Quantum with a 75-foot aerial ladder, 1,500 GPM Waterous pump, and 500-gallon water tank. The rig is powered by a Detroit 470 h.p. diesel engine. Upper windows allowed maximum light into cabs that required tinted window glass in sunny climates. (Chuck Madderom)

Set against a backdrop of Honolulu's skyline, this chrome yellow Seagrave serves the city and county department's Pawaa Station. Ladder 2 was built for Honolulu in 1992 and mounts a 100-foot aerial ladder. It is powered by a Detroit 450 h.p. diesel engine. It is department custom that apparatus are marked with their assigned stations. Despite the region's warm climate, all riders, including the tiller person, are required to be in protective enclosures. (Chuck Madderom)

The San Francisco Fire Department continued its white over red paint scheme along the top of the truck to include the tiller cab. Truck 6, a 1994 Spartan with 100-foot LTI aerial ladder, is equipped with wooden ground ladders, long a department standard. Despite their weight, wooden ladders are safer since they do not conduct electricity. In compliance with NFPA directives, white reflective striping completely surrounds the rig. (Garry E. Kadzielawski)

Powered by a Detroit 450 h.p. diesel engine, this 1992 E-One hush with 95-foot aerial ran with the Town of Brookfield, Wisconsin, Fire Department. A 1,500 GPM pump and 200-gallon water tank provides multi-function versatility. During the 1990s, a number of Midwestern departments began adopting the black over red color scheme. (Chuck Madderom)

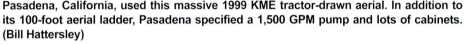

Pasadena, California, used this massive 1999 KME tractor-drawn aerial. In addition to its 100-foot aerial ladder, Pasadena specified a 1,500 GPM pump and lots of cabinets. (Bill Hattersley)

Sutphen aerials are easily identified by their bulky aerial mounts. Truck 1 of the Escondido, California, Fire Department operated this 1998 Sutphen 100-foot aerial tower. (Bill Hattersley)

It was most unusual to see aerial apparatus with front-mounted pumps, especially large pumps rated at 1,250 GPM, such as this unit of Creswell, Oregon. E-One built this rig with three-section 50-foot Strato-Spear aerial on a 1992 International Harvester S Model crew cab chassis. A 500-gallon tank was contained within the truck body. (Bill Hattersley)

FDNY's 21 Truck is one of 32 truck companies, along with 43 engine companies, protecting 1.5 million residents of the borough of Manhattan's 23 square miles. Wearing the slogan "The Pride of Hell's Kitchen" across the windshield, 21 truck's 75-foot tower ladder was built by Saulsbury on a 1997 Seagrave chassis. (Author's Collection)

This rare combination of Pierce Arrow with Marmon-Herrington 4 x 4 was acquired by the fire department of Vail, Colorado. The 1990 unit features a 1,500 GPM pump with 400-gallon water tank. Rear stairs access the 75-foot aerial ladder's turntable. Reflective striping, regardless of color, was required by the NFPA's apparatus standards, beginning in the 1990s. (Dennis J. Maag)

Like many fire rigs of the decade, this E-One Cyclone was built for multiple functions. Serving Hesperia of the San Bernardino, California, Fire Department, the 1999 unit featured a 75-foot aerial, 1,500 GPM Hale pump, 500-gallon water tank, and 20-gallon foam tank. Power was supplied by a Detroit Series 60 rated at 470 h.p. Lettering on the cab's side window memorializes the FDNY's loss on 9/11. Although Federal Q sirens never went out of style, modem versions were fit with a shroud in the interest of preserving the riders' hearing. (Chuck Madderom)

The Alsip, Illinois, Fire Department used this unusual aerial truck, which was built using a 1970 Sutphen body with an extended, fully enclosed American LaFrance Century cab. Attached to the side of the 100-foot aerial ladder is a pre-piped waterway, which was supplied by the unit's 1,500 GPM pump. Although American LaFrance maintained traditional use of its bumper-mounted bell, its trademark bezel lights were reshaped into more angular units. (Garry E. Kadzielawski)

Painted with an unusual scheme of black over yellow, this 1999 American LaFrance Eagle combines an 85-foot LTI aerial with 2,000 GPM pump and 300-gallon water tank for the Highland, Indiana Fire Department. Although low on the color spectrum for visibility, the use of black striping is permitted under NFPA guildelines due to its disruptive pattern and reflective qualities. Making the difference in visibility is the type and arrangement of warning lights. (Garry E. Kadzielawski)

21st Century

Economic woes and subsequent minimum staffing reached an all-time high in the new century, foretelling the future of the fire service. The days of rigs with specific functions and firefighters trained for specific tasks have given way to multi-purpose vehicles with smaller crews that are trained for emergencies ranging beyond fire suppression. The advancement and expansion of Emergency Medical Services (EMS) in the fire service is but one of the major changes that affect fire apparatus design.

While complying with record numbers of safety standards, aerial equipment is larger, stronger, and reaches higher. Aerial platforms in particular, are able to support previously unimaginable loads not only of firefighters, but those imposed by the operation of multiple master streams.

Practicality, more than ever, plays a greater role in apparatus design. For example: attractive, but costly and high maintenance, chrome or stainless steel bumpers have given way to steel bumpers that can be painted, or that can incorporate equipment bins.

Despite the popularity of single-chassis aerial platforms and rear-mount aerial ladders, the tractor-drawn aerial ladder is here to stay. Despite advances in technology and the best efforts of apparatus engineers, the maneuverability and stability of the tillered truck, plus its proven ability to create continuous access to heights, guarantee its continuation as a front line apparatus.

Regardless the direction that the design of aerial apparatus takes, one thing remains certain; their main purpose will be to position firefighters where they can make a difference to those in danger.

Ladder 2 of Hays, Kansas, runs this 2006 Freightliner M2/2007 Rosenbauer-Central States with a 1,250 GPM pump and 75-foot galvanized aerial. Rosenbauer, which began turning out fire apparatus in Austria during the 1930s, used a "hot-dipped" galvanizing process to coat the steel aerial with zinc for anti-corrosion. The rig's cab roof appears as a domed shape, which gave personnel more head room. The aerial's tip nozzle could be controlled from the turntable or manned by a firefighter on the aerial. Extended bumpers often featured vertical rods that helped the driver maneuver the truck. (Dennis J. Maag)

The City of Columbus, Indiana, Fire department ran this 2000 Sutphen with 95-foot tower as Ladder 2. Built into the rig is a 1,500 GPM pump. Typical of the features that firefighters add to their rigs to personalize them is Ladder 2's firefighter caricature on the aerial, a plaque at the base of the ladder control pedestal memorializing the FDNY twin towers disaster, and a Mack bulldog figure mounted atop the radiator grille. Sutphen aerial ladders have long been recognizable by the large pointed section where the hydraulic lifting cylinders are located. (Mark Stampfl)

In November 2009 the St. Louis Fire Department realigned hook and ladder assignments so that each of six districts had one. In keeping with the department's Total Quint Concept, a pair of 2009 Spartan Gladiator Evolutional Smeal quints were placed in service. Both featured a 125-foot aerial, plus 2,250 GPM pump, 300-gallon water tank, and an 18-gallon foam concentrate tank. Hook and Ladder 5, formerly Hook and Ladder 15, shows off the department's new black over red paint scheme. Chrome wheels, black reflective striping, and a white-painted aerial complement the apparatus. (Dennis J. Maag)

This 2006 Seagrave with 100-foot aerial ladder is well stabilized with "H" stabilizers at the rear, and "A" stabilizers behind the cab. A pre-piped waterway is positioned under the aerial's sections. The pale maroon truck runs as Truck 1 of the Leonardtown Volunteer Fire Department of St. Mary's County, Maryland. A time-honored bell and Roto-Ray warning light adorn the truck's cab. (Mike Wilson)

This 2005 Pierce Dash was the only aerial apparatus called an Aerial Tower by the Chicago Fire Department. The 105-foot truck protects the city's downtown South Loop area. Written in gold on the cab door's reflective stripe are the words, "We're there when you need us." (Mark Stampfl)

E-One's Bronto RLP Series is a skylift with closed boom, and telescoping and articulating aerial capable of vertically reaching 100, 114, or 134 feet, plus 88 feet of horizontal reach. An aerial ladder adjoining the boom allows its use as a conventional ladder. Four stabilizers retract into its relatively short wheelbase for maneuverability. Truck 3 of Anaheim, California, is a 114-foot Bronto. Fully stabilized, all of its left wheels are off the ground. (Mario and Trina Silva)

Pierce began building 75-foot aluminum aerials in 2005, and 100-foot aerials in 2008. Truck 22 of Spring Valley Township, Clark County, Nevada, is a 2005 Pierce Quantum with 75-foot aerial, TAK-4 independent front suspension, 1,500 GPM pump, and 500-gallon water tank. It is powered by a Detroit 490 h.p. diesel engine. While the apparatus of certain manufacturers often was concentrated in the geographic region of the builder, Pierce apparatus are dispersed nationwide, given that they are the premier apparatus builder. (Chuck Madderom)

Tower 23 of the Denver Fire Department is this 2005 Pierce Lance 2000 with 100-foot aerial platform. During the new century, Pierce began offering a U.S. flag motif incorporated into the cab grille. Mounted to the front of the basket, or bucket, are two master stream appliances. (Patrick Campbell)

Like many industries, Jack Daniels of Lynchburg, Tennessee, ran its own fire brigade, which included aerial apparatus. The company's 2001 E-One Hurricane aerial platform stretched 95 feet with a basket, and 90 feet with the basket removed. At the aerial's tip is a 3,000 GPM remote-controlled foam nozzle. Ladder 7's unique truck also features a 3,000 GPM pump, 500 gallons of foam concentrate, 500 pounds of Purple K agent, and it has a Williams "Hot Shot" foam system with 500 gallons of Aqueous Film-Forming Foam (AFFF). (Dave Organ)

This imposing mid-mount platform quint was available from KME in heights of 81, 95, or 100 feet. Seymour, Connecticut, opted for this 95-footer built in 2005. The Aerialcat, a trade name carried over from Grumman, included a 2,000 GPM pump and 300-gallon water tank. Tandem axles were needed to support this brute. The height of the tower permitted a stand-up cab. (Lou Tibor)

This eye-catching truck belongs to the Osage Beach, Missouri, Fire Protection District. General built this rig on a 2007 Spartan Gladiator chassis with Rosenbauer/Metz 105-foot Raptor aerial. A Cummins diesel engine powers the rig and a Hale 1,500 GPM pump. Written on the patriotic face of the aerial is the slogan, "Fly'n High & Proud of it." An air conditioner unit is mounted atop the cab. Like early Magirus aerials, a ladder is needed to mount the aerial. (Dennis J. Maag)

Chandler, Arizona, ordered this 2006 Pierce with 95-foot tower ladder and 1,500 GPM pump. A Detroit Series 60 515 h.p. diesel engine powers Ladder 281. Red trim sets off the liberal amount of white used on this rig. The massive proportions of such single-chassis fire apparatus had been inconceivable in earlier decades. (Garry E. Kadzielawski)

Known for its orange fire apparatus, the Coal City Fire Protection District of Illinois ran this 2000 Pierce Dash with 100-foot tower ladder and 2,000 GPM pump. Overall orange apparatus are rare, yet when complemented with reflective striping and warning lights, are easily visible to drivers. (Garry E. Kadzielawski)

Ladder 41 of the Hurricane, Utah, Fire Department sports an Olympics motif, having served at the 2002 Salt Lake City Olympic Games. In addition to its 75-foot aerial ladder, the 2001 Pierce Dash features a 2,000 GPM pump and 500-gallon water tank. Few modern rigs are single-color, with white being the most common second color used with red. Aerial tips are often orange or red to aid in spotting them in smoky conditions. (Garry E. Kadzielawski)

Constructed by Spencer on a 2002 Spartan Metrostar chassis and equipped with a 75-foot R & K aerial ladder, Quint 1121 serves Union Fire & Rescue of Wheeler, Indiana. Wearing the ultimate in patriotic themes, the rig is powered by a Cummins ISL-400 diesel engine, and features a pre-connected flexible suction hose fitted in its extended front bumper. This rig's pump is rated at 1,500 GPM and it carries a 450-gallon water tank. (Garry E. Kadzielawski)

The work of four builders was combined to produce this elaborate aerial truck for the Gary, Indiana, plant of U.S. Steel. The firm 3D Manufacturing built an American LaFrance body on a 2000 Freightliner chassis, with mid-mount 75-foot aerial by Aerial Innovations. Truck 2 also features a 1,500 GPM pump, 500 gallon water tank, and 10 gallons of foam concentrate. Pump connections appear at the rear of the rig, next to the recessed pump operator's panel with roll-up door. (Garry E. Kadzielawski)

The largest tractor-drawn aerial trucks built are those pulling huge trailers with long aerial ladders and ample cabinet space. This 2003 American LaFrance Eagle with 100-foot LTI aerial ladder also has a 1,500 GPM pump and 300-gallon water tank. Power is derived from a Detroit Series 60 500 h.p. diesel engine. Finished in the popular 21st Century scheme of black and red, Truck 31 serves the fire department of Woodinville, Washington. (Garry E. Kadzielawski)

Unusual is the overall black livery of this 2001 E-One Cyclone of Willow Springs, Illinois. Truck 600 has a 1,500 GPM pump and is topped by a 95-foot tower ladder. Yellow cylinders attached to the side of the bed ladder contain breathing air, which is piped to firefighters' SCBA connections in the bucket. Probably the most unusual color for fire apparatus is black, which defies most beliefs about high visibility. The liberal use of warning lights and disruptive reflective striping, not to mention a bright silver aerial, compensate for the black finish. (Garry E. Kadzielawski)

Its ironic that the profile of this ultra modern aerial apparatus bears a resemblance to the German-made Magirus aerial ladders of the 1950s, since this aerial too was made in Germany. This truck was built by General on a 2008 Freightliner M2-106 chassis with 105-foot Rosenbauer/Metz "Raptor" aerial. The German firm Metz became a member of the Rosenbauer Group in 1998. Powered by a Cummins diesel engine, the red and black unit was delivered to the New Berlin, Wisconsin, Fire Department. The basket of the aerial was removable. (Chuck Madderom)

This 2001 Pierce Quantum with 100-foot aerial was one of two ordered by the fire department of Las Vegas, Nevada. Features of Truck 1 include an air-conditioned tiller cab, a Honda 3.5Kw gas-powered generator, and an Opticon traffic signal device mounted atop the light bar on the cab roof. The aerial rests below horizontal to give the tiller driver improved forward visibility. Dark tinted windows for both cab and tiller have become standard for Las Vegas apparatus. (Chuck Madderom)

Wearing an older color scheme, Truck 54 of the North Las Vegas Fire Department is a 2004 Pierce Quantum with 1,500 GPM pump. Above the pump panel is seen a booster hose reel, which is fed by a 500-gallon water tank. Also built in are a foam eductor system for proportioning foam-water mix, and a 10Kw generator. Truck 54's color combination of gray, white, and red forms a livery unique to the Las Vegas area. (Chuck Madderom)

The Greenwood, Indiana, Fire Department boasts this colorful 2006 Pierce Dash with mid-mount 95-foot aerial. Mounted atop its stand-up crew cab is a light bar with clear lenses and an Opticon traffic signal device. Undoubtedly, one of the most striking schemes ever to grace a fire truck, this dramatic scheme in itself is on a par with high visibility markings and warning lights. Dark gray seems to emphasize the tower's sturdy structure, while balance is evident by the white color and chrome wheels. (Christopher Allen)

Rear view of Greenwood's Aerial 91 showing the elaborate artwork familiar to the city's fire apparatus. Twin 1,000 GPM turrets are mounted to the aerial's bucket. This rig's overall size and weight is the maximum for modern aerial apparatus. (Christopher Allen)

Although red is the favored color of fire apparatus, the beauty of this 2008 Seagrave Marauder II more than compensates for the absence of red. The white over yellow Truck 3 of the Bay District Volunteer Fire Department of St. Mary's County, Maryland, has a 100-foot aerial ladder with pre-piped waterway. Sirens are recessed into its front bumper and a Roto-Ray warning light is centered on its radiator grille. A ladder provides access to the tiller cab. (Mike Wilson)

Artwork on the rear cabinet doors of Truck 3's Seagrave show the three trucks previously operated as Bay District's Truck Company 3. Such intricate graphics not only enhance the truck's appearance, they represent the pride of the department. (Mike Wilson)

This 2003 Pierce 2,000 GPM quint with 100-foot aerial tower is one of only two tower ladders operated by the U.S. Marine Corps fire service. (Tom Shand)

After the era of popularity of the color lime yellow passed during the 1980s, few departments used the color, although high on the color spectrum. One exception was Wauwatosa, Wisconsin, which ran this 2003 Seagrave quint with 75-foot "Meanstick" aerial and 1,250 GPM pump with 350-gallon water tank. Quint 3 was powered by a Detroit 475 h.p. diesel engine. Unusual on Wauwatosa's rig is the wraparound stainless steel panel on the cab, and multiple reflective bands. Roll-up cabinet doors were found to be less prone to damage than hinged types. (Chuck Madderom)

The North Middleton Township Volunteer Fire Company No. 1 of Cumberland County, Pennsylvania, runs this 2005 E-One/Bronto 100-foot aerial as Truck 39. Mid-mounted is a 2,000 GPM pump and 300-gallon water tank. Dual air tanks for supplying firefighters' breathing apparatus are mounted to the gray-colored boom. Patriotic cab window and grille dressing became popular during the decade. (Patrick Shoop, Jr.)

During the 21st Century, blue reflective striping came into regular use. Application of the striping, which is required by the NFPA, must include sharp disruptive angles as an eye-catching measure. Espy Fire Company No. 1 of Pennsylvania's Columbia County operates this 2005 Pierce with 105-foot aerial ladder, 2,000 GPM pump, and 500-gallon water tank. (Patrick Shoop, Jr.)

The cabs of Pierce Quantums, which were introduced in 2004, provide room for ten people. The Quantum also offers the most powerful range of engines, from 455 to 515 h.p. diesels. The cab has air-activated steps that extend downward and retract on door opening and closing. This demonstrator was earmarked for the Sacramento, California Fire department. (Pierce Manufacturing)

The Progress Fire Company of Dauphin County, Pennsylvania, operates this 2002 Seagrave with 95-foot Aerialscope as Tower Ladder 32. This is the largest version of the Aerialscope, having the longest telescoping booms, dual tandem axles, and a four-door extended crew cab. Often, fire stations were remodeled to accommodate such massive rigs. (Patrick Shoop, Jr.)

U.S. Steel of Gary, Indiana, is one of many industrial giants that are protected by their own fire organizations. A number of firms came together to complete this durable rig in the year 2000. Truck 2 is a Freightliner chassis built by American La France and 3D Metals. Aerial Innovations provided its 75-foot aerial ladder. Other features include a 1,500 GPM pump, 500-gallon water tank, and 100-gallon foam tank. (Garry E. Kadzielawski)

One of the many pieces of emergency apparatus protecting Pittsburgh International Airport is Truck 19, which is a 2005 Pierce with 100-foot aerial ladder and 2,000 GPM pump. While most airport fire departments are thought to consist mainly of crash-rescue vehicles, they also operate conventional apparatus for structural fire fighting. Dual master stream nozzles and floodlights on the tower bucket have become standard fixtures on modern aerial apparatus. (Patrick Shoop, Jr.)

Mounted high atop this 2006 Spartan is an Allain 75-foot aerial. Allain Equipment Manufacturing Ltd, which was established in Canada in 1976, builds a wide variety of emergency and non-emergency equipment. Truck 204 of the Hualapai Valley Fire Department of North Kingman, Arizona, also features a 1,500 GPM pump, 500-gallon water tank, and Foam Pro 50A foam system. Firefighting tools and a roof ladder are secured in the ladder's fly section. (Chuck Madderom)

The Honolulu Fire department ordered two of these 2001 Pierce Quantums with Oshkosh all-steer suspensions. The rigs have a Waterous pump rated at 2,000 GPM, a 150-gallon water tank, and a Husky foam system, which discharges foam through the tower only. Tower 9 operates from Kakaako Station. Both single-chassis and tractor-drawn aerials serve Honolulu, which has long favored the latter. (Chuck Madderom)

Hartland, Wisconsin, operates this tough truck, which Pierce built in 2000 with a two-door Peterbilt cab. Powered by a Caterpillar 330 h.p. diesel engine, the rig mounts a 61-foot Skyboom aerial and 1,250 GPM pump and 500-gallon water tank. Over its long history. Peterbilt has retained its cab style. (Chuck Madderom)

Winston-Salem, North Carolina, ordered a number of Sutphen SP-70 quints with 70-foot platform. Truck Co. 2's 2001 SP-70 also has a 1,500 GPM pump. Sutphen's distinctive wrap-around pre-piped waterway supplies master stream appliances on both sides of the aerial bucket. (Robert Brackenhoff)

The Paugassett Hook & Ladder Company No. 4 of the East Derby, Connecticut, Fire Department runs this brutish rig, a 2000 Pierce with 100-foot aerial ladder. True to fire service tradition, Truck 15 carries a chrome bell, which balances a rime-honored federal Q siren on the opposite end of the bumper. A Stokes basket is carried atop the cab. (Lou Tibor)

University City, Missouri, operates this 2003 E-One Cyclone II/Saulsbury with a Bronto 100-foot boom and 2,000 GPM pump and 300-gallon water tank. Bronto units often are an exception to aerial booms painted white. Although white is not required by the NFPA, it has become the standard for aerial booms in view of its highly visibility and tendency to soften the hard lines of massive equipment. (Dennis J. Maag)

In 2009, Bullhead City, Arizona, placed in service Ladders 11 and 21, which is an identical pair of Spartan Gladiator Evolution/Rosenbauer Central trucks with 75-foot RK aerial ladders. Both are powered by a 515 h.p. Detroit diesel engine and feature 1,500 GPM pumps and 400-gallon water tanks. (Chuck Madderom)

The long-framed Truck 7 of Eagle Hose and Hook & Ladder Company 6 of the Ansonia, Connecticut, Fire Department is a 2000 Pierce tower ladder. The mammoth rig's Federal siren is recessed into the front bumper and wording across the uppermost cab above the windshield says "Whatever it takes." (Lou Tibor)

A unique blue over red scheme is used on this 2002 American LaFrance Eagle with LTI 100-foot aerial tower. Operated by the West County EMS-Fire District of St. Louis County, Missouri, this unit contains a 2,000 GPM pump, 300-gallon water tank, and 30-gallon foam tank. Dual independently-controlled master stream nozzles have become common on modern fire apparatus. (Dennis J. Maag)

The Pattonville Fire District of St. Louis County, Missouri, runs this engine/ladder unit, a 2008 Pierce Velocity with 2,000 GPM Hale pump, 300-gallon water tank and 95-foot tower. Power comes from a 500 h.p. Cummins diesel with Allison 4000 automatic transmission. Tower 4835 features a diamond tread equipment container in its front bumper. A sign of the times has the department's website address written on the tower's hydraulic cylinder. (Dennis J. Maag)

This view of Bullhead City's Ladder 21 shows to good effect the use of blue for the aerial and reflective trim. An emblem memorializing New York's loss of 343 firefighters on 9/11 is worn immediately behind the cab windows. No artwork on 21st Century fire apparatus has become more prevalent than that paying homage to the tremendous loss suffered by the Fire Department of New York. (Chuck Madderom)

Amid the ruins of New York City's World Trade Center on 9/11, Ladder 163's Mack Aerialscope/Tower Ladder is an enduring symbol of the FDNY's dedicated service in the face of the most challenging of disasters. A total of 19 ladder trucks, along with 25 engines and hundreds of police and fire vehicles, and ambulances were destroyed in the attack. (Author's Collection)